PRAISE FOR *BUDDHA: 9 TO 5*

"Today's leading-edge companies are embracing values and the ideology of *corporate consciousness* to improve their bottom line. *Buddha: 9 to 5* offers a practical and enlightened path for CEOs and managers to transform the communication and profitability of their companies. It is an indispensable tool for leaders driven to do the right thing."

—PATRICIA ABURDENE, author,
Megatrends 2010: The Rise of Conscious Capitalism

"These timeless principles can unlock the gateway to renewed values and prosperity in corporate America. In *Buddha: 9 to 5*, Nancy Spears shows how these principles can help us engender awareness of our intrinsic wisdom, which leads to a higher level of leadership, one rooted in compassion and loving kindness."

—SAKYONG MIPHAM RINPOCHE, author,
Ruling Your World

"Bring together expertise in the most powerful force shaping our material world—business—and a deep understanding of one of the most profound wisdom traditions—Buddhism—and you get this inspiring, pragmatic, and enlightening book. *Buddha: 9 to 5* is an absolute must read for anyone seeking to connect the reality of business and the Reality of Life. It is a transforming read for anyone who simply wants to live more wisely."

—RABBI IRWIN KULA, author,
Yearnings: Embracing the Sacred Messiness of Life

BUDDHA: 9 to 5

THE **EIGHTFOLD PATH** TO ENLIGHTENING YOUR WORKPLACE AND IMPROVING YOUR BOTTOM LINE

BY NANCY SPEARS
Foreword by Sakyong Mipham Rinpoche,
author of *Turning the Mind Into an Ally and Ruling Your World*

Adams Media
Avon, Massachusetts

Published by
Adams Media, an F+W Publications Company
57 Littlefield Street, Avon, MA 02322. U.S.A.
www.adamsmedia.com

ISBN 10: 1-59869-053-1
ISBN 13: 978-1-59869-053-8

Printed in the United States of America.

J I H G F E D C B A

Library of Congress Cataloging-in-Publication Data
Spears, Nancy.
Buddha : 9 to 5 / Nancy Spears.
p.   cm.
ISBN-13: 978-1-59869-053-8 (pbk.)
ISBN-10: 1-59869-053-1 (pbk.)
1. Leadership. 2. Buddhism. I. Title.
HD57.7.S6943 2007
658.4'092—dc22
2006102185

This publication is designed to provide accurate and authoritative information with regard to the subject matter covered. It is sold with the understanding that the publisher is not engaged in rendering legal, accounting, or other professional advice. If legal advice or other expert assistance is required, the services of a competent professional person should be sought.

—From a Declaration of Principles jointly adopted by a Committee of the
American Bar Association and a Committee of Publishers and Associations

Many of the designations used by manufacturers and sellers to distinguish their product are claimed as trademarks. Where those designations appear in this book and Adams Media was aware of a trademark claim, the designations have been printed with initial capital letters.

This book is available at quantity discounts for bulk purchases.
For information, please call 1-800-289-0963.

This book is dedicated with great love and devotion to:

Sakyong Mipham Rinpoche, who teaches me compassion,
wisdom, and spiritual warriorship

My mother, Gwen, who brings heaven to my earth

And to my father, Jim, who has
taught me the essence of integrity.

CONTENTS

PATH TWO
Right Intention: Mission   /   19

PATH THREE
Right Speech   /   40

PATH FOUR
Right Action: Accountability / 62

PATH FIVE
Right Livelihood / 81

PATH SIX
Right Effort / 102

PATH SEVEN
Right Mindfulness / 122

ACKNOWLEDGMENTS

The journey of bringing Buddha to corporate America owes tremendous gratitude and appreciation to many. The bold vision of applying gentle ancient traditions to an aggressive corporate culture to help return ethics and integrity to the working world has been a challenge! It would not have come to fruition without the love and encouragement of many, including the following.

To my brilliant teacher, Sakyong Mipham Rinpoche, who liberates us with his inherent wisdom, moves us with his generosity of heart, and inspires us to rule our world. Thank you for your foreword, your teachings, and your love.

Thank you also to the enlightened Chogyam Trungpa Rinpoche and the lineage of Shambhala, the heart of my spiritual path. With gratitude to Pema Chodron for igniting my karmic path of Buddhism and to Khandro Rinpoche for sharing her discipline of practice and for telling me that I have to write this book.

Also thank you to my precious twins, Clark and Gwyneth, who through their basic goodness awakened my true bottom line; my father, Jim Spears, who has spent his life serving others and who without his love and support my life would be very different; my mother, Gwen, for her legacy of love, strength, humor, and authenticity;

and to Edna Ryan for her heritage of dignity, outrageous confidence, and generosity.

Thank you to my publisher, the Adams Media, and to Jill Alexander for seeing the vision and potential of *Buddha: 9 to 5*. Thanks to Dupree/Miller and Associates for believing in this book and a special appreciation to my agent and editor, Jennifer Holder, for her wisdom, clarity, and tenacity. Thanks to my dear friend Terry Dillman, to John Naber for connecting me to Dupree/Miller and Associates, and to Steve Aldridge for his insight and patience.

Thanks with love and appreciation to my soul mate, Susie Carr, who is a shining example of basic goodness; to Jeffrey Waltcher, for his love and tireless efforts in enhancing my world; to my lifelong best friends, Becky Byrd Lofstead, Diana Getz, Joann Kurtz, and Mindy Vernon; to Betsy Fifield for her examples of generosity and perserverance to change the world for children; to Tom and Darlynn Fellman for their love and support; and to my dear friend, Lexie Potamkin, who shares her lifetimes of values as we raise our twins together.

Also thanks to the creative, highly spirited, and uncompromising staff at Creative Event Marketing (CEM) for your inspiration and dedication, including Judy Salzinger, Nicole Rechter, Richard Sims, Janet Garwood, Julie Kominsky, and Robert Berry. For rich work experiences and growth I thank our hundreds of clients, including Johnson & Johnson, Nike, Time Warner, Eli Lilly and Company,

BMG, AT&T, Toyota, and the Coca-Cola Company. A special thanks to Wayne Stetson at NAHB and Bob Hobart at AMA for getting us off the ground and to Fred McManus at John Hancock and Gloria Mercurio at Lucent for believing in us.

To Rick Murray and to the Inter Public Group for realizing the potential of CEM.

And finally to my loving siblings, Kimberly, Tone, Jimmy, and Maureen, who have never stopped sharing their basic goodness. I am truly blessed to have an abundance of loving, intelligent, and awake people in my life who care about making the world a better place.

FOREWORD

More than 2,500 years ago, the Buddha discovered the key to enlightenment for ordinary human beings like you and me. He then gave us a practical set of guidelines that can lead to genuine happiness. Today, these timeless principles can unlock the gateway to renewed values and prosperity in corporate America. In *Buddha: 9 to 5*, Nancy Spears shows how these principles can help us engender awareness of our intrinsic wisdom, which leads to a higher level of leadership, one rooted in compassion and loving kindness. The confidence and compassion found in these lessons can ultimately benefit all of society.

Over the past few years, I have seen Nancy apply these principles to her own life and business. She is truly unique and unusual in that she remains genuine, compassionate, and intelligent, and at the same time, has had success, both in the business sphere and in her personal life. I'm delighted that she can share her insights, which are not something she has randomly conjured up; they are based upon a long tradition that stems back over two and a half millennia. At this time, her book is critically needed because we live in a business-dominated world. If we can infuse our business with the principles of compassion, wisdom, and mindfulness, then it will have a significant positive impact on others. As we bring these virtues into our lives, we ourselves will be happier people, and ironically, we will become more successful. *Buddha: 9 to 5* is not about short-term success, but about success that lasts, because the best CEO is the Buddha within each one of us.

Sakyong Mipham Rinpoche

THE WISDOM TO WAKE UP

Twenty-five hundred years ago, the Buddha defined a roadmap for living. Today his message can save corporate America from its chaos and corruption and initiate healthy change in the workplace. Is your company awake? Begin to explore what an "awake" organization is:

- Is the quality of communication open, spacious, and motivating?
- Does my company foster a creative, nonthreatening environment for its employees to do good work with passion?
- Is the leadership of my company mindful of its mission and values?
- Does my corporation have a goal that includes making an impact on the world that is for the better?

WHY WAKE UP?

In the twenty-first century, companies make headline news daily by showing us how not to lead an organization. Yet, in the wake of this corruption, astute managers view these lessons as opportunities, and they are transforming their organizations with future, values-based leadership. Perhaps in your own company, you can identify management styles that appear self-serving or are not working. You may intuitively know that it is time to approach business in a new way, to upgrade the quality of communication, in and out of the boardroom.

Each year, CEO's, executives, and managers seek ways to instill leadership that will yield positive financial results and improve employee morale. Yet, few business philosophies offer practical, useful applications to accomplish these goals. Perhaps you have tried the latest management techniques for success, only to receive marginal, short-term rewards. It is time for a new approach, one that you can use every day.

Bringing the principles of Buddha into the boardroom is a unique strategy that can help you to cultivate lasting success throughout your organization. These timeless nuggets of wisdom were given to us nearly three millennia ago by the Buddha. Bringing Buddha into the workplace can become your action plan for long-term reward.

THE BUDDHA: A CEO

The Buddha understood that at our core, each of us is basically good. It is that goodness that enhances our capacity for greatness. From this point of view, all of us are the Buddha. A chief executive officer, senior vice president, or middle manager, in the mindset of the Buddha, can implement a highly effective way of doing business that will transform his or her corporation. As a leader, you foster the application and eventual fruition of that change.

Buddha: 9 to 5 offers tools to identify what you love. Once identified, the next step is to bring that gift into the workplace by communicating it with clarity.

Buddha: 9 to 5 offers a management style that combines your unique gifts with ageless communication tools that empower and engage you and your employees. It is the total integration of heart and mind, or in the words of the Buddha, compassion and wisdom.

When you and your employees are driven by a desire to make a positive impact on your business, and on the world, you experience a commitment that goes beyond a job or career. It is a commitment to service. Our spirit is awakened when we can contribute to something larger than ourselves. A Buddhist master once exclaimed, "You have this precious human body in order to serve other living beings."

In a company that uses the leadership precepts of the Buddha, the process of doing the work itself motivates employees to excel. They know that their work is bringing lasting value and benefit to others, and they are inspired to make a difference. From this point of view, the path becomes the goal and ultimately the means to prosperity.

Entering this path requires working from your inherent intelligence. Wisdom is a noble strength that balances integrity and compassion. This is the consciousness of the Buddha—and the Buddha nature that resides in all of us. This nature is not weak or timid, aggressive or self-serving. When you consciously tap into your own profound wisdom, you communicate and take action from an extraordinary and far more effective place. You reveal who you really are with a powerful presence that fully engages your employees and customers.

THE EIGHTFOLD PATH TO AUTHENTIC LEADERSHIP

The first Buddha, Siddhartha Gautama, gave us a vision, a practical doctrine of values and truths, termed the Eightfold Path. This path was created to help free the world from suffering and obtain enlightenment. He called this enlightenment "waking up." The key to the enlightenment of your organization is The Eightfold Path to Authentic Leadership, a proven model that offers strategic practices to improve the bottom line for you and your company, increasing efficiency, productivity, and creativity.

This first-ever business application of the Eightfold Path provides a practical guideline to values-based leadership and management. It has been developed to serve as a master companion for anyone in the corporate world to carry at work and throughout life. The path includes a hands-on set of tools to raise the bar of authentic communication and interaction in all levels of the workplace from management to the boardroom, from the field to the executive office.

The eight principles of the path are not presented as a step-by-step, progressive exercise. Each of the practices is interdependent and interrelates. The Buddha intended the path to be thought of as a wheel with eight interconnected spokes to guide you through the three essential values of life: wisdom, ethics, and mindful awareness. These values are associated with the following path principles:

WISDOM
1. Right View: vision
2. Right Intention: mission

ETHICS
3. Right Speech
4. Right Action
5. Right Livelihood
6. Right Effort

MINDFUL AWARENESS
7. Right Mindfulness
8. Right Concentration: meditation

The following template or mandala, entitled the "Awake" Corporation Organizational Chart has been created for your everyday use. It provides a visual reminder for you and your company to "wake up."

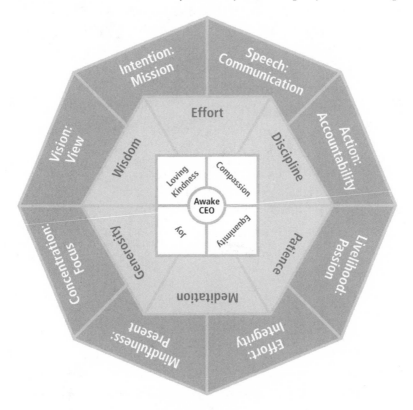

The open space in the center of the mandala represents core values that are constant in the heart of the wheel of leadership. Each spoke represents one of the eight principles and is illustrated in detail. This mandala can serve as your quick daily reference for making bottom-line decisions.

IMPLEMENTING THE EIGHTFOLD PATH TO AUTHENTIC LEADERSHIP

As you progress along the path, you may begin to notice changes in how you deal with intense situations or that you measure success with a different criteria. Perhaps your decisions are more spontaneous or your interaction with others is more open and less guarded. You may find that your bottom line is not based solely on a healthy P&L, but on a strengthened intention within your company to do what is right. The timeless quality of the path provides you with immeasurable tools to reawaken your company, again and again.

Wisdom Training

Strengthening, focusing, and calming the mind is an important first step to accomplishing any goal. Many teachers speak of this process. Sakyong Mipham Rinpoche, master teacher, global spiritual leader, athlete, and author of the national bestseller, *Turning the Mind into an Ally*, and the award winning, *Ruling Your World*, refers to this process as training the mind. Essentially, we are training our minds to see our truth.

We train in wisdom both externally and internally:

Externally, as a leader, we train by exuding level-headedness, showing that we are decisive but reasonable. We are discerning about all aspects of our business, not just the financial bottom line, but also the well-being of our employees, stockholders, and those with whom we do business.

Internally, our wisdom is revealed with deeper insight. As we access our internal wisdom, we cultivate warmth, integrity, and gentle strength. We release our fixation on ego and turn our mind outward. That helps us to understand others, and through that understanding, we create value in our organizations.

We develop compassion through our experiences, and often the most painful phenomena also bring us the deepest connection to others. A vice president of a leading global technology company discovered the value of appreciating and learning from others following the tragic death of his sixteen-year-old son. He used his grief and suffering from the loss of his precious child to take his company inward and consciously explore how to interact and manage differently in order to make a difference. In the process of opening to others in his company, he learned to let go of judgment. This enlightened style of management, inspired by his trust in others, earned breakthrough results that the VP ultimately equated to contributing millions to the company's bottom line.

Managing with internal and external wisdom creates a balanced and more meaningful style of leadership. Because you are more aware of your employees' needs as well as those with whom you do business, you can groom an organization that is in touch with the world and its needs.

RIGHT VIEW: VISION

"Unattached to speculations, views, and desires, with clear vision, such a person will never be reborn in the cycles of suffering."
—The Buddha

THE RIGHT VIEW

Right View, the first principle in the Eightfold Path for Authentic Leadership, mindfully connects you with the real world. It is the cornerstone that reminds you to see the world as it is: exquisite and intense. In business terms, the Right View is the vision you hold for your organization. When a potent vision threads into every goal and step of a company's path, it sustains the corporation and stimulates growth.

With Right View, we wipe the dust from our eyes in order to focus clearly on what is and how we can relate to that reality. We see what we are up against, not what we want to believe will happen. Can you see yourself and your company as you really are today? Do you understand its differential and why and how it stands out in the market?

Can you visualize its true potential and maintain a realistic handle on what it will take to transform your organization, to wake it up?

One insight into understanding your company's potential is to know how people close to your company describe the organization. By directly relating to your customers' and employees' opinions about your business, you are able to keep a finger on the pulse of your organization's positioning and potential growth in the marketplace. This connection enables you as an entrepreneur to find innovative ways of doing business that in turn benefit your customers and industry.

Barbara, a senior vice president in the technology industry, prescribes grassroots activism and think tanks to get to the root of her company's positioning. According to her, "Radical tools and change principles occur first inside the walls of our company, which then enables us to move outward." Today, her inward to outward vision is bringing life-changing technology to developing countries.

Leading with the Right View requires being present in every situation. When you have Right View, you communicate and listen with insight that is clear and unobstructed. The Buddha saw this clarity as our wisdom. How do you access it? You create it by having a vision that connects your thoughts and actions to your company's immediate and long-term success. Project your success by visualizing the specific outcomes that you and your company will experience as a result of holding to the Right View. Do you see your employees motivated and eager to exceed your customers' expectations? Does that vision translate to greater profitability and a stronger, sustaining organization?

ACCESSING THE MOMENT

This book offers twenty-two exercises that can train you to stay in the present moment. In the wisdom of the moment, you experience the greatest change in your bottom line. It also provides you with staff path practices, tools that help you to work with your staff on the same principles to increase your bottom line.

Mindful Awareness
EXERCISE 1

Take a few minutes to reflect on these Right View questions:

- What is the long-term vision of my company?
- What is its purpose? What impact does it have on the world?
- What are the basic values of my organization? Am I aligned with these values?
- What areas do I need to investigate in order to realign with my organization or to take action to change it?

Contemplating these questions is an exercise in training internal wisdom and helps cultivate the Right View for you and your organization. You can return to this exercise whenever you sense the need for a realignment of your view, or a reassessment of your Right View.

CEOS WITH THE RIGHT VIEW

When Phil Knight formed Nike, his view was to connect everyday people with great athletes and accomplishments, by just doing it. When Oprah Winfrey launched her daytime TV program, she had a view to empower women by giving them the tools they need to access their intelligence and talents. And, when Bill Joy founded Sun Microsystems, he was driven by a dream to improve computer technology in business, and he is now referred to as the "Edison of the Internet."

Each of these visionaries far surpassed their personal and corporate goals by holding to the Right View. With explicit awareness, you can create a view and a mission for your company that will withstand the barriers of time, policy, and struggles in the marketplace.

Having the Right View helps access the intelligence of your corporation as you connect with your employees and customers. It's that connection that will ultimately drive the strategies that improve your bottom line. Phil Knight and Oprah Winfrey are master teachers of how to connect their visions with their employees and consumers. Consequently, the turnover rate and attrition levels in these cutting-edge corporations is low. Their employees like to show up for work and season their company's contribution to the world with their own unique talents. They identify with, and commit to, the company's vision. Do you see parallels with these stories and your organization?

In order to begin to appreciate your company's view, ask yourself the following questions:

- Are your employees, managers, and customers connected by an integrated, unified vision? What is that vision?
- Does the climate of your company empower people to tap into their own special talents?
- Does your company encourage its employees to realize their own dreams through their jobs?

With vision-based leadership, you engage your intuitive intelligence in order to peer into the total capacity of your organization. It is at this point that you can define your company's values, mission, and long-term purpose. You know what makes your organization stand out in the marketplace, in the world. That knowledge stems from a wisdom that provides the basis for awakened management.

THE WRONG VIEW

In the mindset of the Buddha, the concept of Right View is quite simple. It starts with a basic awareness of what is truthful and right: right for your employees, right for your customers, right for the world.

Leadership motivated with the Wrong View can ultimately drive a company into bankruptcy.

Today, we are experiencing the emotional and financial damage of Wrong View leadership throughout corporate America. Although executive offices concerned solely with increased profits and bonuses may be able to survive in the short term, their ability to set long-term, effective strategies will be futile without the Right View.

The fear of failing or not having enough originates in the ego. Wrong View is cultivated by positioning yourself as the primary benefactor of your dreams. It is the fixation on "I" that generates fraudulent or insincere actions and ultimately can lead to a spiraling breakdown of an organization.

Focusing on the "I" is not vision-based leadership and has led to the breakdown of many companies who had the potential for abundant success. This breakdown was demonstrated in one of the premier entertainment companies in the world, the Disney Corporation. Founded by Walt Disney, a creative genius whose vision was to make people laugh, this corporation held to its vision as a pioneer in animated cinema. But when the leadership was turned over to the next generation, the focus shifted to increasing the wealth of a few executives at the top of the food chain. The wealthier these CEOs and COOs became, the harder they pushed for profits and greater shareholder returns. Their obsession stifled the company's creativity, which in this case was its product and ultimately led to the breakdown of the company. On the verge of bankruptcy, the board of directors finally requested the resignation of the CEO and other officers and refocused the leadership on the company's core vision. Today, with Right View, the corporation is back to the business of generating innovative creative products, which, in turn, is revitalizing its bottom line.

By simply shifting the focus from "I" to "other," you begin to explore success from a different point of view. Your leadership motives should include knowing what is in the best interest of your employees, customers, shareholders, and the world. This view connects you with the wisdom of every employee in your company and defines the path toward greatness, a greatness that goes beyond salary and net worth.

Jim Sinegal, the CEO of Costco, one of the world's largest and fastest growing discount retail chains, is proving the benefits of internal generosity and placing the needs of its employees and customers first. Sinegal wears a name badge that reads, "Jim." He is on a first-name basis with his 4,000-plus employees and is on a mission to prove that good guys can finish first—and without all the corporate frills. In an era when profits continue to rise to the top, Sinegal is breaking new grounds of modesty by paying himself a $350,000-a-year salary, a fraction of the millions most large corporate CEOs make.

This CEO is unfazed by his critics and holds to his vision of maximizing staff retention and creating a company that offers value to its employees. "Wall Street is in the business of making money between now and next Tuesday," commented Sinegal in an article in the *New York Times*. "We're in the business of building an organization that we hope will be here fifty years from now. And paying good wages and keeping your people working with you is good business." This CEO has proven that a company doesn't have to be greedy to be successful. Being humane and holding to your view can make you money.

ESTABLISHING THE VIEW

Right View is the first step in the Eightfold Path to Authentic Leadership because it forms the foundation for how you communicate both internally and externally.

When I formed my company, Creative Event Marketing, my view was to impact the lives of our employees, clients, and their corporations by delivering positive strategies and insightful services that exceeded their expectations. To accomplish this task, my vision was to minimize our vulnerability by cross-pollinating our client base and strengthening our creative expertise in a variety of industries. This strategy gave our employees the confidence that we could withstand downfalls in specific markets and maintain long-term financial stability. This view provided the opportunity for our company to cultivate an environment in which to develop creative product. It was this vision that grew the business. Ultimately, I sold it to one of the leading marketing conglomerates in the world, the Interpublic Group.

There are five factors that measure the effectiveness of your company's Right View (see the Mindful Exercise below).

STARBUCKS

IN 1981, STARBUCKS COFFEE WAS a Seattle-based coffee bean store whose simple vision was to hand select and sell excellent coffee beans. While the business was quality based, it lacked the vision required for growth and global expansion.

However, director of marketing and operations Howard Schultz had a different view. He also wanted to "build a company with soul." The conservative owners resisted, and Schultz went off to create his vision before returning in 1983 to purchase Starbucks for $3.8 million.

Schultz became the CEO and chairman of the board of a global company that by 2006 achieved gross sales of $4.1 billion. As Schultz grew the business, he consistently held to a vision to establish the company as the premier purveyor of the finest coffee in the world. Schultz also had a view that it is possible to be successful while maintaining uncompromising principles, even with growth.

He backed up that view by forming six guiding principles that would help the leaders of the company measure the appropriateness of their decisions. These six principles are:

1. Provide a great work environment and treat each other with respect and dignity.

2. Embrace diversity as an essential component in the way we do business.
3. Apply the highest standards of excellence to the purchasing, roasting, and fresh delivery of our coffee.
4. Develop enthusiastically satisfied customers all of the time.
5. Contribute positively to our communities and our environment.
6. Recognize that profitability is essential to our future success.

Schultz also embraced the company's employees and secured their loyalty by going ahead and implementing a series of practices that were unprecedented in retail. He insisted that employees who worked a minimum of 20 hours a week and their partners (married or not) receive health care benefits. Schultz then introduced a stock option plan that actually reduced employee turnover and increased productivity, despite the low pay standards prevalent in its industry.

This demonstration of holding to the Right View has resulted in a company that has boosted employee morale and, in turn, brand loyalty to a global operation that boasts climbing sales averaging 20 to 25 percent a year since the company first went public.

When asked the secret of his success, Howard Schultz declares, "Compromise anything but your core values."

ESTABLISHING THE VISION

Once you see your vision and believe in it, you begin to cultivate an awareness that cannot be ignored. Extraordinary energy propels you to take your organization to the next level.

Establishing your vision begins by going within to identify your gift. The employees at Starbucks deliver a dependable positive experience for their customers. They are motivated by the vision of the quality of product and service that they offer. It is this vision that allows them to experience their jobs from their own Buddha nature.

Every manager in corporate America can access this potential in themselves and their employees. Most business people spend at least 70 percent of their day working or thinking about work. For many, they are dispassionate about this great deal of time. Yet, with vision and clear view, your leadership qualities can begin to unfold. Ask yourself:

- What are your gifts?
- What is your personal career vision?
- What is your company's vision?
- How do your talents translate to your company's vision?

Although this exercise is an intuitive process, for many it is not spontaneous and can be stifled by the hard-edged boundaries of a department or entire corporation whose goals are focused on short-term gains. For example, Mark was a loyal, talented marketing manager for one of the world's leading beverage companies. Daily, he worked to build the brand and position his company at the top of its industry. His ability to relate directly to the marketplace created cutting-edge ideas that directly affected beverage sales and increased the shareholder returns. Mark was invaluable to the company, and yet few in the company were aware of his contributions, even after twenty years of service. Mark's boss was on a mission to earn every promotion and pay increase possible, even if it meant taking the credit for Mark's efforts. The structure of the corporation allowed this to happen quite easily. Discussions of top-level brand positioning were confined to the boundaries of the boardroom and executive office. The employees that sparked the creativity to drive that positioning were kept behind the scenes, with little recognition of their ideas.

Mark eventually left to work for a more progressive company that appreciated his gifts and encouraged him to present his ideas to its senior management team. Today, Mark also sits on the executive committee, charged with building a branding team and recruiting innovative talent that can see the company's products with fresh eyes.

Adapting policies that openly encourage the creative input of your employees will cultivate an open and highly motivated environment in which to effectively transform your company to an enlightened state. In order to lay the ground for this spacious work environment, it is helpful to implement a practice that helps you and your employees to access your creative visions. A simple practice to free the mind will soften your competitive edges, liberate your daily performance, and result in dynamic external change.

A PATH PRACTICE FOR RIGHT VIEW AND VISION

Have you ever looked out at an ocean and focused only on the crashing waves, losing sight of the exquisite horizon line? Similarly, turbulence in the marketplace, employee trauma, attacks from competitors, and other disruptions at work can all interrupt the clarity of vision.

With pressures encountered on a daily basis, holding to the Right View can be slippery. Establishing a practice that clarifies vision will help retain the focus needed to manage your business strategies effectively. Just as your products or services are strengthened by your continuous efforts to improve their quality, so will the clarity of your vision be sharpened by practice.

Whether it is daily or weekly, the more consistently you evaluate your decisions to ensure that they are aligned with the Right View, the more productive and values-based your management style will become. Eventually, this strategic discipline will intuitively engage your awareness of the view, and right decisions will be made consistently, on the spot. This clarity comes with practice!

The Practice

The following practice provides you with a template from which to go within and analyze the position of your company in order to initiate change. Having said that, the essence of the Right View practice is to detach from the outcome of the practice long enough to access your

Mindful Awareness
EXERCISE 3

Select one of these exercises and do it for as many days or weeks as you feel necessary.

- Contemplate the current climate of your company. Is it positive, neutral, or in pain?
- Visualize what your company would look like if it were free of distress and worry.
- Contemplate the qualities of your company that stand out from the competition.
- Honestly answer: Is my company contributing to the welfare of others?
- Ask yourself: Does my company genuinely care about the needs of our employees and our customers? Do I?

Regularly returning to the same contemplations with an open mind will breathe space into your habitual mindset and allow you to see things from fresh angles and perspectives, including seeing all sides of a situation. You will know when a shift in view occurs.

core thoughts and values. Your goal is to seek your honest feedback and evaluate whether or not your views are aligning with your vision.

At the beginning of each week, take the time to clarify your Right View with this practice. Sit in a quiet area without distraction. Select from the following contemplations or create your own Right View practice in order to connect to your employees, customers, and the marketplace.

MINDFUL ACTION STEPS

The following steps can further help you to keep your heart and soul connected to the pulse of your business.

- Call or visit an existing customer for candid feedback on your products or services.
- Schedule an out-of-office meeting with an employee to learn more about his or her understanding of the vision.
- Exercise the tried and true MBWA (management by walking around) policy. Ask a lot of questions and listen not only to what your employees answer, but to the tone of their responses. Do you sense apathy and burnout or enthusiasm and passion for what they do?

BUDDHA'S COMMENTARY

By bringing Buddha thinking into the boardroom and workplace, you make a choice to expose your basic goodness and inherent wisdom. In so doing, you are primed to elevate your corporate consciousness with compassion and values-based leadership.

Be aware that his process is not quick, easy, or painless. But the long-term results will prove to be enormous. As the process of waking

Staff Path Practice

With each path, this book provides you with useful tools that will help you to implement these practices with your staff. In Buddha's terms, this is referred to as "practice in action" and it is truly where the results are demonstrated on a company level. With each path, the model is consistent but the specific direction relates to the path in discussion. The three steps for implementing Right View/ Vision are:

Strategic practice: Meet with your staff as a group, calling upon each of them to participate throughout the exercise. Recite or give them a copy of the company vision. Feel free to paraphrase it. Ask the question, What is your vision of your job? Of your career?

Tactical practice: Open a discussion on how the individual's vision integrates or conflicts with the company's vision. How do they speak to each other?

Operational practice: Brainstorm what you can do better as individuals, as a department, and as a company to fulfill this vision.

up unfolds, you will eventually notice a refreshing change. Your employees will be engaged and excited to tap into their own strengths and creativity with deeper levels of commitment. This change will be reflected in your products, services, company culture, and bottom line.

RIGHT INTENTION: MISSION

"Correct all wrongs with one intention."
—Atisha Dipankara Shrijnana

THE RIGHT INTENTION

By instilling the *Buddha: 9 to 5* approach to management, you make a choice to take the high road and elevate your corporate consciousness with deliberate intention. You decide to examine and fine-tune corporate and personal missions. In essence, you commit to set the Right Intention and to wake up your organization.

When you and your employees carry a sense of commitment that is driven by an intention to make a positive impact, you cultivate a personal power that goes beyond the job itself. You set a tone of confidence and dedication that stems from the root of your mission, the Right Intention. It is this intention that drives the day-to-day effort and ignites excitement in the workplace.

Once ignited, your company's mission will serve as a beacon that illuminates the way to making healthy decisions. You and your employees can focus on the work itself with a newly kindled inspiration. By tuning in and establishing an awareness of your intention, you will seed a path that flourishes with inspiration and prosperity.

Having the courage to walk this path requires working with your inherent intelligence and genuine basic goodness. Our wisdom, our intelligence, is what we often refer to as the "little voice" that we hear in the back of our mind. Although we frequently opt to ignore it, the voice is always present and can be accessed at any time. It is pure, luminous and unbiased. It tells us what is real. It is our wisdom. This wisdom is the consciousness of the Buddha nature that resides in all of us. When we access this nature, we are said to be waking up!

Mindful Awareness
EXERCISE 4

Begin to set the Right Intention with a few tough but honest questions. Ask yourself:

- Does my company offer a motivating, creative, open environment for employees to do good work with passion?
- Are our employees committed to making a difference by contributing uniquely to the success of our company?
- Does this organization function as if it is awake?

THE FOUR IMMEASURABLES OF A LEADER

The foundation of your mission statement should represent your core qualities. Buddhism provides us with a practice that calls up these qualities and provides a template for the core of your mission. Termed the Four Immeasurables, the practice generates a genuine ability to soften and broaden your view about your place in the world, and therefore access your Buddha nature. These four qualities serve as your nonnegotiables and are the core of your mission. The Four-Immeasurables in the context of Buddha in the workplace and boardroom are:

Loving Kindness

When we relate to our self or another person from a place of loving kindness, we ask for happiness to surround them and us. The loving-kindness practice affirms: "May all beings enjoy happiness and the root of happiness."

When we consciously declare thoughts of loving kindness, we connect with our authentic self to cultivate that success and happiness. In the business model, this quality requires that we work with a positive intention to serve ourselves and others in the organization ethically, generously, and with kindness. In situations that involve negotiations, loving kindness takes off the edge of aggression and clears the way for open communications.

Compassion

Compassion is the conduit to increasing the growth of your organization and for impacting the world. The basis of compassion is to stay open enough to feel the pain or needs of others, which expands your view beyond your personalized, absorbed self.

When you access your compassion, you communicate from the heart, and that communication transcends the borders of hierarchy and position to allow for the flow of effortless creativity. As you write your mission statement with a mindset of compassion, you can see how your efforts in human resources, sales, research and development, customer service, and so on contribute to the health of your organization and the world at large.

When a mission statement demonstrates compassion, a natural cycle of prosperity is created. The CEO and board direct the organization with values and genuine caring, which in turn motivates the employees and enhances productivity and which ultimately increases profitability and growth. This cycle of management by compassion then flows full circle back to the shareholders, CEO, and board.

Joy

When you practice a joyful mindset, you delight in the happiness and success of others and eliminate the need or temptation for jealousy and aggression. Joy promotes a vibrant work culture internally and externally. When you and your organization practice joy, you ask that, "all beings not be separated from their own happiness, free from suffering."

In this sense, the mission and values of the organization acknowledge a goal to enjoy prosperity and success and to use the benefits of that success responsibly and with integrity. Thus, this practice guards against the risk of the inappropriate use of profits, pension plans, and other improprieties that would negatively affect the employees, management, and shareholders of a corporation.

Equanimity

Equanimity allows us to accept the good and the bad in all situations; having the peace of mind that everything is workable. When managers engage the quality of equanimity, they establish a motivated work environment that engages everyone in their department or company. Equanimity also provides a workplace free of prejudice or discrimination, and this freedom encourages open-minded thinking and cultivates innovation.

In this practice we ask that, "all beings dwell in equanimity free from passion, aggression, and prejudice." Equanimity is an essential condition of a values-driven mission. It expands the possibility for growth and opens the doorway to attracting new talent and knowledge that will be recycled into the organization.

The Four Immeasurables provides the foundation or centerpiece of the *Buddha: 9–5* mandala. Take a look at the chart on this page. The chart illustrates the equality and balance of the Four Immeasurables that we have been discussing in this chapter.

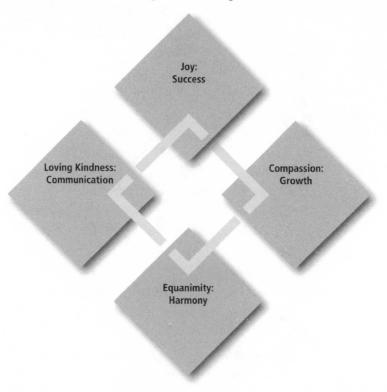

Joy:
Success

Loving Kindness:
Communication

Compassion:
Growth

Equanimity:
Harmony

How do each of the quadrants look in your own work practice or environment? Integrating the Four Immeasurables into your daily awareness practice at work will strengthen your organization's communications and increase its productivity and vitality.

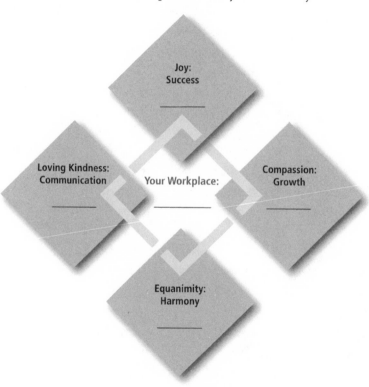

COMPANIES AND CEOS WITH THE RIGHT INTENTION

Former *Washington Post* publisher Katharine Graham once said, "To love what you do and know that it matters, what could be more fun!" A secret to leading with Right Intention is to love your work. When you believe in your company, service, or product and know that it makes the world a better place, your intention stays crystal clear.

Intention is the censor of our thoughts. It is what determines the quality of each action, each moment, each life experience. Each experience can be steeped in pleasure, pain, or ambivalence. We inhale the pleasure of landing a promotion and bask in the sweetness of our company's rising stock prices. In a split second, without warning, we realize that this joy is short-lived. The pleasure abruptly changes to pain, as we are passed up for a much-desired promotion or watch our stock value plummet.

Because we choose our intention, we are also in control of our experience. Leaders who understand this principle are poised for greatness, both in and out of the workplace. Executives who maintain Right Intention can withstand the neurotic quality of the marketplace and let go of the constant craving for momentary success. In the back of their minds and pit of their hearts, they know that everything is workable. That knowledge evokes a confidence that enables them to stay focused and on course with their views and their missions.

With the pressures of our speedy corporate world, how can you keep your intention alive and accessible? By applying tools and skills that help to sharpen the awareness of your intention, you can stay connected with your mission. The first tool that helps to realize your intention is to possess a genuine love of your work. When you love your work and openly express a desire to make a difference, you tune into the voice in your heart that inspires you to lead with a conscience. You also commit to the quality component of your mission that, when sharpened, can produce stunning results.

Lou Gerstner, retired CEO of IBM, emphasized the critical quality of integrity in corporate culture. Gerstner is a textbook example of consistently leading with the force of Right Intention. He was known

Mindful Awareness
EXERCISE 5

You can use the Four Immeasurables to create a mission statement for your company.

- List the values that you feel are essential to the livelihood of your organization.
- Place the values in the appropriate quadrant of the *Buddha: 9 to 5* Four Immeasurables on the worksheet provided.
- Notice any areas that are void of values and explore cultivating that quality to strengthen your company's authenticity.
- Refer to your list of values and write or rewrite a mission statement for your company.

for referring to the IBM mission and challenging his managers to push the envelope both creatively and with good, old-fashioned work ethic. His personal work practices were recognized by *Fortune* magazine, which credited him with adding more than $40 billion to IBM's market value in just four short years. Perhaps *Fortune* should have recognized others on the IBM team who worked tirelessly to achieve this success, but it was Gerstner at the helm who pushed for cutting-edge products, leading-edge service, and profits in a dynasty that will go down in corporate history as the flourishing model of "Big Blue."

Yet, you don't have to lead a global technology empire, save an entire rain forest, or invent the cure for cancer to make an impact. While these accomplishments are remarkable indeed, even the most modest contributions, when driven by Right Intention, are significant. By sharing your creativity to bring a product to market, helping colleagues hit their departmental goals, or simply taking the time to listen to another when you are under the pressure of a deadline, you exemplify Right Intention. Regardless of the size of the task, when we stay tuned into our intentions, we intuitively make the right choice. Our reactions in the moment are far more appropriate and effective. Events that once raised the hair on the back of our necks now go unnoticed or perhaps even bring an inward smile.

Another tool that helps us to access our inner voice, our Buddha nature, is Virtue. Virtue is the barometer that keeps our intentions in check. Virtue involves reaching into our compassion, our concern for others, aligning ourselves with our vision and our values. We all have the capacity to tap into our virtue at a moment's notice.

Some could say that lack of virtue tore the heart out of corporate America during the scandal epidemic of this century. Virtues that brilliant, talented leaders were born with were compromised for short-lived fame, fortune, and in many cases fictitious profitability. The good news is that while many leaders lost sight of their Virtues, it is always there, ready to be recaptured, instantly.

Virtue is synonymous with Right Intention and mission. It is the rudder that directs intention. Without virtue, we cannot stay on course. We are simply spinning out with the need to win at all costs, while our genuine intention is lost in a fog of self-serving desire.

Virtue is another way of understanding our Buddha nature. It provides the ground for our awareness and simple decency as human beings. It is our virtue that provides the bottom-line clarity to define our mission statement.

THE RIGHT MISSION

Awake management begins with the mission. The leadership and management of an awake company is mission driven. What does this really mean? We hear statements like: "They are on a mission," or "Hold to your mission," and we take these as rhetorical clichés. But if we examine these words closer, we find that a mission actually speaks to the values, heart, and passion of an organization and its employees.

Companies such as Johnson & Johnson, Coca-Cola, and John Hancock all endured difficult times with remarkable sustainability due primarily to their ability to hold true to their missions. A corporate mission describes the organization's passion, authenticity, and potential to make a positive impact in its industry and in the world. Good, sustainable missions incorporate values, codes of ethics or

Mindful Awareness
EXERCISE 6

Whether you are crafting a new mission statement or reengineering your company's existing credo, consider the following:

- Does your mission state why your company exists?
- Does it list the reasons why you are in business such as: enhancing the world through XYZ product, improving the lives of employees, maximizing investments for stockholders, etc.?
- Does it describe how your company serves the world?
- Does it succinctly describe your corporate values?
- Does it incorporate messages of virtue?

virtues, views of how to help or enhance the world, and quality statements that get to the heart of the company's existence.

Self-sustaining companies use their missions as roadmaps to make healthy short- and long-term decisions. Those decisions are driven by a knowing awareness of the cause and effect of the company's actions.

Yet, investing sizable amounts of money and time into creating a mission statement for a corporate culture does not guarantee success. Unfortunately, far too often mission statements become merely boardroom wallpaper.

How can you ensure that your company's mission statement will not become dispensable? You can do this by keeping it clear, brief, and accessible to everyone in your organization and with whom you do business. Your company's mission statement should be so precise that it speaks to every employee, while so broad that it touches the world.

When your mission statement succeeds, it becomes your corporate path. It should become the credo by which your company's leaders manage. It should be firmly rooted in the hearts and minds of your CEO, VPs, and staff since it is the doctrine by which they make decisions.

Johnson & Johnson was my company's client for more than a decade. The Johnson & Johnson executives were inspiring, motivating, and exciting to work with. Regardless of how challenging the assignment or difficult the request, I always wanted to do whatever it took to deliver great work to them.

When dealing with Johnson & Johnson, I always knew that my company and our employees would be treated intelligently and fairly and that the results of our efforts would make a difference in the world.

Why?

Because the leaders at Johnson & Johnson live and work by their credo. Day to day, moment to moment, management instills the mission statement, values, and leadership they inspire in the lives and hearts of their employees. Another company that shared the same value basis and virtues driven by its mission was the Ritz Carolton Hotel Company.

THE BUDDHA'S MISSION

The Buddha delivered a "mission statement" more than 2,500 years ago that is far-reaching and succinct: "To help liberate all sentient beings from their suffering."

Examine just how timeless this statement really is. It declares the compassion that is needed in all organizations even today. Why? In the broadest sense, missions that emphasize the welfare or benefit of others allow for the recycling of generosity and prosperity.

Today, a mission statement that focuses on adding value to the lives of others and the world, rather than for the shareholders exclusively, will prove to be much more sustaining and prosperous for the organization and in return, the shareholders. Your mission statement is your mantra for work. A mantra is your company's guiding principle aligned with your guiding vision.

Everyone in the company from the CEO down throughout the organizational chart lives by the mission. Missions should be discussed constantly and used as a benchmark not only in the boardroom, but also in department meetings, client presentations, and at employee reviews as a vehicle to authentically inspire your workforce and customers.

The Buddha's mission was to help others. Through his spiritual awakening, the Buddha determined that one's line of work or rank does not determine the level of "success" of a person. Rather, a person derives happiness through commitment, value-based actions, spiritual growth, and knowledge.

By writing a personal mission statement, you strengthen your core beliefs and values and pledge your commitment to help others in your life. Likewise, within your company, you promise to serve your employees and customers with integrity and purposefulness.

If you are not in a position to rewrite your corporate mission statement, then perhaps compose a departmental support statement as a way to restate your commitment or write your own personal mission statement.

Regardless of the hierarchy in place, by pledging to focus on your bottom-line purpose, you strengthen your intention and position your company to be able to make a difference. Additionally, when every member of your organization is in sync with the same goal and purpose, the result is improved loyalty, teamwork, and, ultimately, increased productivity.

THE PRACTICE

You must recognize that this practice is not quick, easy, or painless. Yet, the long-term results will prove to be enormous. As the process

Mindful Awareness
EXERCISE 7

Take a few minutes to reflect on these questions to connect to your company's mission:

- What is your company's mission statement?
- Is the mission statement current and in alignment with the present values of your organization?
- How do you demonstrate this mission? What are some examples of your "practice in action" at work?

of waking up unfolds, refreshing changes will occur. Employees will become engaged and excited to tap into strengths and creativity at deeper levels of commitment.

Contemplating these challenging questions will help to reconnect you with your organization's mission and its Buddha nature. By looking within, you have begun the task of clearing your path toward waking up your personal management style and thus your organization. This book will provide you with succinct tools that will help to strengthen your communication skills for long-term profitability both personally and professionally.

Staff Path Practice Challenge your staff with the following path practice:	**Strategic:** Deliver the company mission statement to your staff. Ask them to break it down into its primary action steps.
	Tactical: Evaluate each step and rate yourselves on how well you follow the core values of the statement at work. What are your strengths and where can you do better as a company and as individuals?
	Operational: Brainstorm and implement three ways to keep the core values of the mission statement at top of mind with your group.

BUDDHA AND THE CEOS MISSION STATEMENT

A personal mission statement can positively affect your daily management style. Your personal mission statement provides the ground for your intention and adds clarity to each decision that you make. Does your mission statement capture the sustainable values that can impact your employees, your organization, and the world in a healthy, positive way?

Your mission statement should have the following qualities:

Authenticity: Representing your company's core values and the heart of its success

Limitlessness: Freed of boundaries that encumber growth and creativity

Timelessness: Withstanding the test of time and evolution of products and services

Generosity: Stating a positive contribution to the employees, customers, and the world

If your company has a mission statement, compare the one that you wrote to the actual statement and identify any areas that are missing but you feel are essential to your company's sustainability and contribution to society.

If you are a manager or department head, consider using these exercises as a basis for writing an internal mission statement. Engage the participation of the employees on your executive committee or within your department to write and commit to the mission statement. As a CEO, you may also suggest this exercise to your managers or executives.

To be in Buddha nature is to be awake and alive. How different would your workplace be if your management style consistently communicated from a place of absolute truth. Imagine the clarity and productivity that could arise.

RITZ-CARLTON HOTEL COMPANY

Every day at 9:05 A.M., at each of the fifty-nine Ritz-Carlton Hotels around the world, CEOs, managers, and employees line up to proclaim their intention to live up to the company's credo. Ritz Carlton takes their credo to the most personal, one-on-one level—to each of its 28,000 employees.

The credo declares: "The Ritz-Carlton Hotel is a place where the genuine care and comfort of our guests is our highest mission. We pledge to provide the finest personal service and facilities for our guests who will always enjoy a warm, relaxed, yet refined ambiance."

Bill Johnson acquired the first Ritz-Carlton hotel in 1983, in Boston, Massachusetts. At that time, the property had the exterior complexion of a sterling, expensive luxury hotel but lacked the universal personal service that distinguishes Ritz-Carlton today. Johnson pondered, how do you bring the concept of elegance inward . . . to the soul of the employees and guest experience?

Enter CEO Horst Schultze and his infamous motto, "We are ladies and gentlemen serving ladies and gentlemen." This motto permeates throughout the company and has set the tone of exemplary service that has earned the hotel chain the Oscar of quality, the Malcolm Baldridge Award. As late as 2007, Ritz-Carlton is one of only two American corporations and the only lodging company to have ever won the Malcolm Baldridge Award two times. This is even more impressive when you consider that companies cannot apply for the award for five years after winning. With a clear intention to lead from the heart of the mission statement, Schultze successfully injected spirit into a culture of quality that permeates the Ritz-Carlton experience.

What is the differential that defines the Ritz-Carlton's approach to customer service over other successful, revenue-driven hotel products? Ritz Carlton employees strive to execute their jobs flawlessly, not because they have to for their annual evaluation and pay increase, but because they genuinely want to.

The intention starts at the root of the credo by personally engaging the employees as "ladies and gentlemen" and empowering them to take the initiative to service their customers with the same style of elegance that their products convey. This process is taken to an employee level that is unmatched in the hospitality industry. All Ritz-Carlton employees carry Ritz-Carlton's "Gold Standards" of customer service printed on pocket-sized, laminated cards.

In an industry with an annual average turnover rate of 55 percent and bottom-line priorities that are measured by gross profit margins, average room rates, and bed night occupancy levels, Ritz-Carlton has found a way to inject empathy into the workplace. The proof is in the results, as Ritz-Carlton boasts a 28 percent employee turnover rate—among the lowest in the hospitality industry.

RIGHT SPEECH

> "There's nothing more advanced than communication . . .
> compassionate communication."
> —Pema Chodron, *When Things Fall Apart*

RIGHT SPEECH

By bringing Buddha into the workplace, you are cultivating compassionate communication. By being grounded by Right View and Right Intention, you are poised to apply the ethical strategies essential to lead from a wakeful place. The first of these ethics and the third path of the Eightfold Path is Right Speech.

Refining the skill of Right Speech provides the compassionate edge that we need to make a genuine change in the world. It is a path that is essential to improving the bottom line of any organization.

Admittedly, practicing Right Speech in a society laden with corporate and government scandal, media hype, and global chaos presents a challenge.

The use of the Internet has further hardened our communication styles, as we are conditioned to craft and send e-mails that are overtly succinct and lack empathy in an effort to get through our work. Many of us have experienced repercussions of thoughtlessly pushing the send button on an abrasive or curt e-mail. Yet, when we choose to be more mindful of how we interact with others and scrutinize the delivery of our thoughts, we can begin to soften our edges. By shifting the focus of our thoughts from me to you, the possibilities of deepening our communication skills expand. Life becomes much more interesting!

With an awareness of others, you can learn to take the emphasis off of yourself and your own small schemes, goals, and desires and focus on a much bigger view. The process of compassionate communication involves the engagement of other human beings in order to be effective and real. It requires us to penetrate a vein of honesty with fearless conviction and expose who we are. In the mindset of the Buddha, there is a place within us that has never been damaged or soiled, a place where tranquility, courage, forgiveness, and unlimited imagination dwells.

When we access this space within, we exert Right Speech by simply speaking the truth. Truth is what helps us to maintain clear focus in order to deliver the impeccable expression of our thoughts and ideas. This expression is direct, genuine, and clear. When we deliver our thoughts with scrutinized clarity, our management style becomes much more effective.

In today's complex business world, brimming with confusion and distraction, how do we stay out of the gray and communicate with black-and-white clarity? How do we consistently speak the truth?

We begin by training our minds.

TRAINING IN RIGHT SPEECH

"We train in not being afraid to be a fool."
—Chogyam Trungpa Rinpoche

It is amazing how many executives do not authentically communicate who they really are. They are frozen in an identity camouflaged by a title or position that blocks their access to their greater potential. We see this fear-based behavior everyday—in the media, in politics, and on Wall Street.

It is only when we lose the fear of being exposed, the fear of failure, that we can open ourselves to our genuine truth and set a new standard of honesty and prime ourselves to speak with seamless clarity.

To understand the nature of authentic communication, we begin with the obvious. When you look up and say, "That is the sky," you are clear. So is everyone else who you say this to and who also sees the sky. After all, you don't say, "That is my sky, but you don't see the sky." We all hear and process the same statement about the sky.

But when you say, "This is a great company because we care about our employees," it gets a bit gray and fuzzy. What are the qualifiers for this statement? Is it really true? Does your company really care about its employees and, if so, how is it shown?

By training in Right Speech, you learn to cut down on the gray or ambiguous words that you select. You begin to discriminate your thoughts and focus on integrity and the reality of the moment. This process requires you to be more discriminating in your thinking and the words that you select to express yourself. It is this clear, direct style that can affect change and the bottom line of your organization in a positive, long-lasting way.

Training in Right Speech helps you to become intimate with what it feels like to communicate with truth and clarity. You can begin with simple steps that vividly connect you to that feeling. By associating with the precision that resonates in your mind and heart when you say an undisputed statement such as, "That is the sky," you are training in the discipline of clear communication. With practice and awareness, you transfer that same clarity to more complicated statements such as, "Our products are superior because . . . "

EGO AND RIGHT SPEECH

Honest communication involves surrendering our attachment to who we are and who we think we are. We have to be willing to let go of our solid identity and trust that a bigger experience, a more open exchange of ideas, is obtainable. We must be willing to free-fall jump into a level of communication that exposes all of who we are, our talents and our vulnerabilities, in order to get to the core of genuine communication. This is the crux of Right Speech.

Losing the ego, especially in a corporate environment, is quite difficult to do. We hold onto it like a security blanket, allowing the comfort zone of ego to protect us from criticism, confrontation, and the fear of realizing who we really are. But the protection is a glass wall ready to be shattered. Rather than protecting you, your ego exposes your fears and insecurities and opens you up to deeper pain.

When you let go of ego, you have room to breathe. You cultivate the confidence to engage Right Speech. When we let go of who we think we are, our inner gifts of intuition drive the communication process. The result is a sense of freedom, connection with others, and accomplishment. We are no longer preoccupied with what others think about us, and we free ourselves to motivate and lead with a fresh approach. By not being afraid to be a fool, you can become a genuine leader.

MINDFUL SPEECH: A PRACTICE

The key to delivering effective, genuine communication is to be mindful of the quality and the speed of your thoughts and how they are articulated. Cultivating mindfulness is a practice in itself.

Mindful Awareness
EXERCISE 8

Explore the following exercise designed to help strengthen your communication at work and elsewhere in the world:

- Devote an entire day to listening to what you say and how you say it without effort to change your communication style.
- Observe your word selection. Write down specific incidences when you are direct and when you make excuses to avoid conflict. Notice times of hesitation and what comes up. Is it fear or confusion? Can you identify the confusion? Can you expose your fear? Do the confusion and fear dissipate or get diluted simply by noticing them?
- Observe the reactions that you receive from employees, colleagues, customers/clients. How open and receptive are others to you? Do you feel avoided? If so, notice your feelings. Is any of the interaction with others uncomfortable and stressful? If so, identify what makes it so.
- Contemplate your word selection and how you delivered your thoughts. Were you manipulative, aggressive, or passive aggressive? Under what circumstances did you lean on these habits?
- Are you able to speak your truth freely and without hesitation?

We cultivate mindfulness by training our minds to stay present and aware. When we are present and mindful, we can observe the emotions and speech patterns of others and ourselves with a bit more clarity. We can catch our continuous distractions of thoughts and be present for others. At last, we can communicate eye-to-eye, word-to-word, without distraction or the pressure of anticipating our own response.

Mindful Awareness
EXERCISE 9

Try this group-based exercise to release ego on the next project that involves communication with your team, colleagues, or employees:

Rather than struggling with the same familiar procedures and agenda items in order to produce a certain result, make the process of communication the project itself. Free yourself from a specific outcome and "hand over" the challenge to the group. Approach the job with a level of openness that actually makes you feel uncomfortable.

Communicate by asking others in the group open-ended questions free of your bias. Encourage people who typically do not participate to do so by asking for their opinions and ideas. Invite employees to the process who are not directly involved in the project.

For example, if you are discussing the consumer marketing of a new brand, invite the controller or a member of the accounting department to brainstorm in the creative process. Mix it up, have fun with it, and experience the difference. By exploring the process itself, you may generate an outcome that is far more effective.

Do you communicate with your employees, customers, and stock-holders with a sense of value and pure intention? Practicing Right Speech is often difficult because our words reveal our thoughts. So when we speak from the heart, we put ourselves out on a limb, exposed and vulnerable. Yet, it is this raw, naked communication that engages us to participate and to initiate change.

FINDING THE "SWEET SPOT" IN COMMUNICATION

Genuine communication involves finding the "sweet spot" that con-nects us to others. The easiest and most direct way to enjoy that con-nection is to release our insistence on being right. When we fixate on an outcome, we close our minds and hearts to other solutions. We grasp on to what we think is the correct and only way, blocking all possibility for learning and growth. This insistence on winning blocks our creativity and stifles the communication process.

When we let go of thoughts and preconceived agendas and open up to the desire for pure communication, we begin to truly listen. We look at the process from a posture of "what can be," and we actually hear more than our own responses. Genuine listening involves seeing and feeling the situation from another person's point of view, even if we don't agree with them. By hearing what the other person really says, we can respond with clarity of truth and begin to speak from the heart. In effect, we sit on the same side of the desk as our "sparring" mate, engaging in an open conversation that is infused with honesty and tempered with kindness and mutual respect.

This open exchange of creativity, which ultimately leads to inspired solutions, is the sweet spot in communication. Reaching the sweet spot is not contingent upon the mutual agreement of an outcome. Growth and progress can be obtained simply by indulging in the process of open exchange. Once there, equipped with a newly discovered ability to tap into our truth and soften the heart, communication skills are primed to blossom. In the context of the Buddha's teachings, that ability has always been there, ready to be accessed. We simply had to slow down long enough to realize it.

LEAP

The formula for consistently nailing the sweet spot of communication is to LEAP: listen, explore, appreciate, and present. The LEAP technique slows down the communication process enough to make it authentic and, therefore, truly effective. By breaking down the procedure of two-way communication, we begin to hear and respond with appreciation and genuine honesty. We learn to repress our task-oriented, aggressive tendencies to shoot from the hip in order to consistently make leaps of progress in how we interact with others in the workplace. Here is the LEAP prescription for curing any damaged communication habits that you may have acquired.

Listen

Listening is the soul of all effective communication. Authentic listening requires the ability to engage your senses. You hear not only what the person is saying to you, but you also see their emotions through their expressions and feel their words through their body language.

By using your sixth sense of mindfulness, you employ the essential ingredients of empathy and compassion. When you listen from your heart, you open to the possibilities of growth and expansion. You are open to your unlimited potential.

Explore

Exploring authentic listening includes asking questions, similar to the process of discovery. When you ask questions, you also reinforce that you are hearing what is being said and setting the pace for two-way communication. This process of "exploring" by asking questions helps to create the space needed to flush out all concerns and get to the root of the issues. In order to explore effectively, it is important that we listen with empathy.

Appreciate

Listening with focus and compassion intuitively enables us to appreciate the viewpoint of the person we are talking to, whether we agree with his or her opinion or not. Genuine exploring requires a desire to understand the other person's position. We ask questions that break down the conflict and open up the issue to its core. This exploration process may last for quite a long time and can even occur over the course of many conversations. By exploring, we further communicate from the heart and demonstrate that we care about reaching a compatible solution. We convey our pure intentions.

To demonstrate appreciation, you simply acknowledge that you heard what was said to you, either verbally or with a gesture such as a nod. This sends out the following message: "Your opinion matters, and I hear what you are telling me." Showing appreciation for others and their points of view sends a message of respect. Conveying a subtle acknowledgment of what has been said helps to break down any barriers that may exist and pave the way for a peaceful, more desirable outcome.

Present

Having engaged in truthful listening, genuine exploration, and empathetic appreciation, you are poised to present your point of view with authentic, wakeful presence. You have earned the trust of the person with whom you are communicating and can now employ the ethics of Right Speech to obtain extraordinary results.

By consistently using these techniques of listening, exploring, appreciating, and presenting, you demonstrate the genuine kindness that leads to a special connection with others. When we communicate

---

Mindful Awareness
EXERCISE 10

Take the LEAP to discover the sweet spot of communication:

- Think of a difficult communication issue and a person with whom to have the discussion.
- Think about listening with compassion.
- Develop questions that will explore and engage the other person.
- Ask questions that unravel any confusion and ultimately get to the heart of the conflict. Acknowledge that you have both heard and understand their point of view.
- Once you are satisfied that you have asked enough questions to understand the other person's point of view, then present your view with conviction and truth.
- Now, look at the issue with a newfound appreciation.

with compassion, we speak from our highest consciousness. As we sit back and enjoy the process, all we have left to do is trust.

THE CAUSE AND EFFECT OF RIGHT SPEECH

When we bring Buddha into the boardroom, we also understand the cause and effect (karmic ramifications) of our speech. By examining the raw truth of a thought with the understanding that every word we choose and every sentence we express affects the outcome of a situation, we can immediately see and appreciate the karmic conditions that we create with our speech. Seeing this pattern helps us to streamline our visions with honest clarity, and communication becomes more effective. As we tap into our wellspring of wisdom and compassion, our communication begins to change. Our words ignite the action that will follow.

In today's competitive, goal-driven work environment, we often find ourselves confronted with challenging communication hurdles. We can be provoked by our colleagues, bosses, or clients to prove a point or defend a position that to us seems quite logical. At this point, our defenses kick in, in an effort to be right or to "win" or simply be heard. Our perception is that by being heard and winning the argument, we will be more successful. What drives this mindset? How do we get so stuck in our thoughts and opinions and create a communication barricade between others and us in our organization? It is our attachment to our thoughts and the ego that supports them. More times than not, these speedy thoughts are not helpful and in fact will damage our bottom line success in the long term.

SPEECH AND THOUGHT

Our speech is obviously reliant on thought. When our thoughts are discursive or speedy, randomly jumping into and out of our mind in an impulsive pace, we lose sight of our vision. Stepping onto this treadmill of thought is not helpful. The speed of thoughts creates an undertow of emotion that can affect what we say and how we say it.

However, you have a choice. You can stay attached to your thoughts, tightening around them and fighting them to exhaustion, or you can give in to the possibility of new thoughts, or even more radical . . . no thought at all!

By stepping away from a situation for a few minutes, you surrender to a decision of "no thought" long enough to irrigate the challenge at hand. This process of "no thought" provides you with the ultimate space you need to find relief. As leaders, we are more effective when we maintain a fluid, flexible mind. This fluidity keeps us creative and in the moment. We are more responsive to the needs of our organizations and can view circumstances with dexterity and fresh eyes.

The Buddha said, "Thoughts are as inherent to mind as waves are to water." Just like we cannot hang out on the same wave forever, neither should we cling to one thought. If our thoughts are so prolific, then why do we hold on to those that keep us stuck? Why not let our thoughts go and allow the next set of solutions to enter our mind?

When we cultivate the ability to allow our thoughts to come and go, recognizing them as only thoughts, we actually widen our view and vision. The tempo of our thoughts accelerates, and we increase our ability to lead with creativity. In essence, we expand our mind with multiple solutions rather than narrowing it with an attachment to one idea.

By letting go and allowing the fluidity of our thoughts to support us, rather than own us, we can eventually ride the waves that will carry us safely to shore.

HOT SPOTS: THE LIABILITIES OF RIGHT SPEECH

In order to wake up an organization, reengineer how we communicate, and free ourselves from confusion, it is helpful to understand the hot spots that block our success. The Buddha referred to these as kleshas, or mental poisons. In a business context, the hot spots are liabilities that directly affect our bottom lines. When we are unconscious of them and they have free rein over our mind and speech, these kleshas have the power to poison our environment completely.

There are five root liabilities that prevent us from accomplishing successful, positive communication. These include:

- Desire or grasping
- Aggression
- Delusion or ignorance
- Arrogance
- Envy

Can you think of examples of times that one or more of these liabilities or kleshas affected your work environment? How have they prevented you or your organization from obtaining goals sooner or with greater success?

Let's examine each hot spot to better understand the impact your company feels when such an emotion prevails.

Desire or Grasping

When grasping rules, whether it is a promotion, salary increase, or approval from a board, we want an outcome so desperately that we mentally cling to the desire. In fact, we may become so obsessed that the majority of our thoughts and conversations at work focus on this subject and our desired outcome. This obsession negatively affects our productivity. Grasping distorts our ability to see any other view or solution around an issue. It blocks creativity, and although we may very well obtain our desired outcomes, we may also forfeit the opportunity to cultivate teamwork and long-term potential.

The best way to prevent grasping and free the way for a creative environment is to catch yourself in the moment of desire and evaluate your motivation. Is it ego based? Is there another way to resolve the issue, or is this truly the only solution? Is the outcome in the best interest of the total company?

This "bottom line" approach to discovering the root of your thoughts will sharpen your awareness of the thoughts themselves and ultimately deliver quicker, more positive, and effective solutions in the work place.

Aggression

Aggression comes in many forms. We feel aggression toward competitors, coworkers, and other board members. Aggression stems from our initial thoughts or reflections on the "enemy." The enemy can be a competitor or someone in your organization who challenges your opinions and decisions. The best way to neutralize thoughts of aggression is to see the sameness in you and your aggressor. They may use a different style or approach, but their desire to win, to be heard, and to succeed is similar to your own.

Try flipping roles in your mind with your opponent in order to genuinely assess the conflict. By actually evaluating their perspective, experiencing their point of view, and feeling their aggression toward you, you can see the similarities in yourself and them. The process is subtle and requires a temporary unbiased view of the situation. You may not believe in their core beliefs or be driven by the same motives. Yet, by mustering up the bravery to examine the similarities in each of you, you can begin to experience a sense of letting go.

When you find yourself in an aggressive position, take a look at the action itself and examine your body language, speech, and thoughts around it. Are they serving you well?

Delusion or Ignorance

The fast pace of our business culture often eliminates the luxury of thoroughly evaluating the challenges that come our way. Day after day, week after week, we are pressed to make decisions, with little time to dig deep for solutions. We rely on our intuitive nature, our experience and, sometimes, sheer luck. We train ourselves to master this "ready, fire, aim" approach to decision making, and it generally serves us well.

Occasionally, we lose our footing, however, when we ignore reality and attach to the illusion of how we would like things to be. We don't look at how things actually are, but hope for an outcome and then make a wishful decision.

The key to working with ignorance is to take the time when available to catch your propensity to make an impulsive decision, step back and broaden your vision in order to view the total landscape that is in front of you. This scrutiny of your thoughts heightens your potential for clear, honest communication.

Mindful Awareness
EXERCISE 11

By examining the source of your liability, you let go of negativity and preserve your sanity. Examine each of the following liabilities in the context of your business or position:

- Desire or grasping
- Aggression
- Delusion or ignorance
- Arrogance
- Envy

Working with Right Speech, this exercise can take you to the edge of your liabilities and help to lead to a higher state of communication, a more compassionate exchange between you and others.

Arrogance

Arrogance is a reflection of our ego and perhaps the greatest obstacle to our success.

Feel the contrast between arrogance and benevolence for yourself: Think of a situation that pushes your button of identity, a position that you take very personally. Perhaps it is the power that you have over others or the respect that your position brings you from others.

Are there also thoughts of overt pride or arrogance that arise? Examine the raw qualities of the arrogance. How does it feel? What goodness will it actually bring to your own personal growth and availability to others?

Now think of a situation that evokes benevolence and kindness. Perhaps it is handing out bonuses to your staff or simply thoughts of a son, daughter, or grandchild. Do you feel less intense and aggressive? Is your mind more spacious and confident?

With benevolence you know what to do. There is no confusion. This is the state that as an awake manager, you want to return to, again and again.

Envy

Most of us deal with envy on a regular basis. We perceive an aspect of someone else's life to be better than our own. Whether it is more money, time, love, or good health, we yearn for more. There is always something that we don't have that we want. We chase through life with an unharnessed excitement to have it all. Driven by achievement and desire, we lose sight of our long-term goals and ignite an ambition to be better.

Staff Path Practice

Everyone in your organization can and will benefit from the application of Right Speech. Take the time to work with your staff on these Right Speech exercises and notice the immediate results:

Strategic: Tell your staff that you are working on cultivating a deeper practice of communication, one that involves open, genuine dialogue. Tell them that you realize that in the haste of getting the work done, we all cut corners in how we communicate with each other. Inform them that you want to improve the communication in your workplace and ask them to help you by participating.

Tactical: Introduce the LEAP method of communication and show them by direct example how it requires the concentration to really listen and to be present. Now ask your staff to think of an example of a stressful or challenging situation that they would like to solve through effective communication.

Operational: Examine the results as they unfold over the week and evaluate them in the next follow-up meeting with the staff. Break down the steps and learn from what worked and what aspects of the communication still need improvement.

Envy stems from a sense of other. The mindset of us versus them, me versus others hardens our thoughts and makes our mind less pliable. A colleague earns a promotion, and we want it. Another company is gaining market share, and we want it. Our competitor designs a new product, and we want it.

How can we break free from this imprisoned realm of envy and ease the burden of jealousy? Although complete freedom from envy is never fully obtainable, you can bring a sense of relief by being more discriminatory about your thoughts and speech. By questioning the point of wanting something, or the importance of earning a specific achievement, you can ease your internal struggle a bit.

Practicing Right Speech in a culture that is controlled by the myths of achievement, power, and product is not an easy task. At the deepest level, by working with your personal assets and liabilities, weakness and limitations, you can discover your true nature.

RIGHT ACTION: ACCOUNTABILITY

> "Having decided to take the direction of virtue, we move forward with joy."
>
> —Sakyong Mipham, *Turning the Mind Into an Ally*

RIGHT ACTION

The path of Right Action suggests that we pay attention to our actions and understand their consequences. In the most basic sense, it reminds us to walk our talk and to treat others like we would like to be treated. Right Action relates directly to the karmic law of cause and effect. In business terms, karmic law is known as accountability. In an awake organization, accountability drives our actions. When we are accountable to ourselves, our employees, our communities, and the marketplace, we make decisions and take action from a place of consciousness, rather than as the pawn of our ego's desire for personal gain. Accountability requires that we replace our "me"–focused mindset with one that addresses the needs of others. In essence, we close the gap between ourselves and others to net a richer, more potent, and far-reaching profitability.

When our circle of accountability expands to include our employees, customers, and strategic partners, we feel generous and softer at heart. This generosity becomes a motivator for going to work every day. Accountability no longer is a task or obligation, but rather a spontaneously creative priority for how we conduct business. And that is what motivates the actions that produce high bottom-line results.

Every action that we make involves a choice. When our actions arise out of virtuous decision making, we choose to take the most efficient, beneficial road toward our goals. Actions that are driven by virtue disempower the hierarchy found in intimidating and often corrupt top-to-bottom management. When the focus of a company is to deliver returns to all of its employees, not just the cream at the top of the corporate ladder, productivity—and therefore profitability—increases.

Clarity of vision, genuine intention, and using Right Speech to eloquently deliver your views offer management the stable ground needed in today's rocky corporate climate. Having cultivated the skills needed to access these tools at a moment's notice, the next true test is to back these paths up with Right Action. Your actions are where the rubber meets the road. They are your demonstration of integrity and the actualization of your karma, the bottom line cause and effect of the decisions that you make and implement daily.

Accountability must flow from the top of the organizational chart downward. When executives of healthy companies implement actions that result from assuming personal responsibility, they reduce the chance for internal chaos within the business.

Why? Simply, they are laying their motivations, intentions, goals, and methods out before the entire organization and stating, by example, that they are accountable to everyone. In this regard, the law of karma then suggests that employees will follow suit and focus on their own actions with greater awareness and transparency. The entire situation becomes more workable and easier to manage. The results are potent.

WRONG ACTION: LIMITED ACCOUNTABILITY

When a corporation loses its accountability, the results are much different. On the surface, a business can have all of the right components to win in the marketplace, but without accountability the actions easily become inconsistent, inflexible, and neurotic.

Consider the situation Lucent Technologies faced in 1996 on the cusp of the Olympic Games in Atlanta, Georgia. Lucent emerged out of AT&T and was predicted to shake up the telecom business with its new optic technology. Dozens of former AT&T executives transferred their years of tenure and pension plans over to the hot new company predicted to quake the industry. With the muscle of AT&T behind it, everyone was purchasing Lucent stock. Just out of the gate, Lucent was already delivering rising stock prices at a rapid pace that shook Wall Street.

But, as their stock soared, the executives began to lose touch with the marketplace. Focused on their position on Wall Street and their retirement accounts, few had the foresight to watch competitors such as Nortel and Alcatel. They inherited the long-term, secure, but sluggish mindset of AT&T along with the speedy confusion of a technology start-up. These traits were overshadowed by a confident arrogance that camouflaged incompetence and the stress of pressure to perform.

The successes and failures of an organization originate at the top. At Lucent, the actions taken by CEO Richard McGinn were motivated by a need to drive up the company's stock, rather than to maintain a competitive edge in the fast-growing telecom marketplace.

It did not take long for competitors such as Nortel to begin taking action and eclipse a large piece of Lucent's market share. What evolved was textbook corporate history on how to ignore reality and take advantage of a base of employees who had genuine intentions to take their jobs and their company to the next level.

Lucent had the advantage, the resources, and muscle of AT&T; the research and development team to deliver brilliant products; and the employee base to make it happen. What they lacked was the foresight and long-term vision that come from virtue-driven actions.

Had the senior management of Lucent been more focused on the growth of Lucent over the long term rather than their immediate desires for short-term success and early retirement, the results could have been much different. Rather than delivering peak and valley returns that damaged stockholder confidence, those in command could have created an organization that drastically changed the standards of the telecom industry. Their bottom line would have been blockbuster.

VIRTUE

Virtue is the internal censor of our thoughts that keeps our action pure and genuine. Virtue keeps us from polluting not only our own rivers, but also our companys'. When driven by virtue, accountability helps us choose Right Action and allows us to "move forward with joy," as Sakyong Mipham Rinpoche says.

As you may have discovered, your attitudes and experiences constantly change. This is part of being human. Each experience can be steeped in pleasure, pain, or ambivalence. We inhale the pleasure of success and bask in its sweetness. Then instantly, without warning, we realize that this joy is temporary as we are faced with the next tough challenge. We need the stability of our virtue and accountability to steady our responses to thoughts and to prompt Right Action.

Virtue involves tapping into our innate compassion for other beings and for our common plight. It is the lingering emotion we experience after a sweet smile from a dear friend or the compelling feeling of positive eye contact with a stranger. We have the capacity to tap into our own virtue, our own basic goodness, at a moment's notice.

Applying tools and skills that help us to sharpen our awareness of our attitudes can produce stunning results. When we are aware, we can choose our attitude in the moment. To that extent, we are in control of our experience. When we choose our attitude, our reactions in the moment also dramatically change.

Virtuous Decision Making

Can you recall a time when you made a decision motivated by desire, duty, or attachment to an outcome? Whether we make a quick decision based on an impulse to better our own situation or just to get the work done, we have all made choices that we could have scrutinized in greater detail by exercising a bit more patience.

The Buddha suggests that when making a decision, we turn toward our virtue and do what we know in our gut to be right. Daily, we are challenged to loosen our attachment to personal gain and accept our moral responsibilities. When we are attached to an outcome, it is nearly impossible to make a decision that creates long-term benefits.

Virtue, on the other hand, keeps our action uplifted and motivated. With a confident spirit we become inspired—rather than intimidated, pushed, or tempted—to take action and exert ourselves to make life happen. It is our attitude that determines the quality of each moment and experience. These same mindsets direct and shape our actions.

NON-VIRTUE

My company, CEM, had a client who was an executive with a global insurance company. Richard was the victim of self-serving management decisions that could only result in disappointment for one if not all of the executives involved.

Richard had been with the company for more than thirty years, during a time of great change and turbulence in an evolving, competitive marketplace. As the years turned over in rapid succession, Richard was placed in compromising situations that challenged his innate desire to do the right thing. He frequently found himself in circumstances that forced him to make choices that were not necessarily in the best long-term interests of the company's bottom line.

These decisions involved providing expensive perks for the company's leaders, extravagant requests that were outside of the boundaries of company policy. Richard, although quite high on the corporate ladder, was coerced to support decisions and people whom he did not believe in. He was forced to choose between taking the safe but faint-hearted path of pleasing others, and the braver, riskier path of leaning into the sword of conviction and doing what was right. Time and time again, he took the path of least resistance, with one eye always focused on the security of his eventual retirement.

The outcome was painfully predictable. Richard became ill. By keeping his bosses and the chairman happy, he compromised his own integrity, and his physical health, by internalizing his misguided actions.

Richard honored the comforts of a few executives at the top rather than the organization as a whole. This lack of veracity blocked the access to his own dignity and immobilized his ability to consistently take the Right Action. Not only did Richard suffer, but his company failed to profit from a proper use of his talent.

As leaders, CEOs are required to regularly take the action needed to support their principles and demonstrate their dominant positions in the marketplace. Knowing when to take action is often the greatest challenge. There is a fine line between strategically thinking through the implication of a decision and timing the follow-through

PROCTER & GAMBLE

Few CEOs of *Fortune* 100 companies have consistently led with Right Action like Procter & Gamble's A. G. Lafley has. Lafley successfully navigated P&G through the wakes of difficult times that have historically damaged and in some cases sunk less secure organizations. What can be attributed to his impressive tenure and accomplishments? At the top of the list is Lafley's keen ability to make purposeful decisions and to back them up with Right Action.

Among those decisions was launching a series of acquisitions that vaulted P&G into a $68 billion-a-year global enterprise. Pulling the trigger on deals such as the $54 billion deal for Gillette requires confidence and the courage to take action.

When Lafely took the helm at P&G in 2000, the giant corporation was flailing with an expensive infrastructure that was not supported by its revenues. P&G was at a critical stage, where despite its strong brands, it had received two consecutive profit warnings in one quarter.

Lafley immediately began to take action. The first thing he did was to take his strategy on the road and communicate directly with P&G customers, employees, and suppliers. For 100 days he exercised Right Speech by asking the right questions and listening to the response in the field. "We had outstanding people, who weren't really clear about the one or two things that would make a difference," stated Lafley in *Chief Executive* magazine.

Lafley took the action to clarify the priorities at P&G and offer solid direction. In addition to the acquisitions, he eliminated the internal confusion by reprioritizing the company's focus on its core brands. This action simplified the highly diversified corporation and gave its employees a grounded sense of security.

In just six years, Lafley provided the 135,000 employees at P&G with a renewed motivation, by implementing right action. The company is awake and operating with a renewed clarity and improved bottom line. As recognition of the change, A. G. Lafley was unanimously chosen the *Chief Executive* magazine 2006 CEO of the Year. In response, Lafley returns the accolades to his employees by commenting, "My job is to unleash the creativity, initiative, leadership and productivity of P&G people. They are the leaders who've delivered the results of the past five and a half years, and it's on their behalf that I accept this recognition." Another demonstration of using Right Speech to back up the Right Action of a true Buddha in the boardroom.

to accomplish its maximum impact. The path of Right Action provides the CEO with the skillful intuition to know when to strike and enjoy the maximum benefit. Timing Right Actions over the long term is vital to the sustainability of an organization.

ATTACHMENT

The Buddha considered attachment to cravings and desires to be the root of pain and suffering. He maintained that in order to be free of suffering and to experience the joy of enlightenment, we must detach from our propensity to always want more.

The question then becomes, how can we detach from our own greed and still be successful in our competitive culture? We find the answer in loosening our attachment to short-term outcomes and focusing on the path, which is the work. When we stay with the process itself, we can let go of our obsession for a success that is measured purely by profitability. We begin to work with the possibility of finding joy in each project, each interaction. By acknowledging the opportunity for multiple solutions in most challenges, and allowing the space needed to discover those solutions, we begin to cultivate a flexible style of management.

As we create a spacious environment for our employees to interact and flourish, we loosen our attached grip. We free ourselves to stay present in the moment and clear our minds to focus on the work. The result is a quality of growth that goes beyond our goals and expectations. It is genuine success.

DO SOMETHING DIFFERENT

As intelligent, capable, accomplished leaders, why do we get so stuck? How do we create our own misery? We usually design our own roadblocks to happiness and success through attachment to an identity, such as the title or position we hold, or to our attachment to a specific outcome. In Buddhism, this attachment is referred to as "Shempa."

When we experience Shempa, we generally will tighten around a thought or concept and eventually we are hooked to that idea. We are stuck. The attachment paralyzes us from seeing issues in any context that is different from our own view of the situation at hand. We are unable to act from a perspective that is open to the creativity of a new approach. As we continue to push the envelope and fixate on the outcome, we are actually building momentum toward attachment. This very inflexible mind is referred to as "Shempa Logic."

FORCED TO DO IT DIFFERENTLY

The manager of a marketing department at a leading telecommunications company had his eye on a promotion for months. The majority of his efforts and actions were strategically managed to prove his worthiness of the new position. Each day, he was presented with another opportunity to showcase his abilities.

However, while focusing on his own desire to be promoted, he neglected to notice the disharmony that was cultivating within his own organization. His fixation on his personal goal had distracted him from noticing the needs of others. An undertow of apathy was brewing while he was lost in his own personal agenda.

Eventually the internal discord became so obvious that it began to affect the performance of the entire marketing department. This decline in performance eventually began to reflect poorly on the manager, and it appeared that his promotion was at risk.

When it was no longer possible to ignore the state of his team, the manager was forced to turn his attention to his employees. He shifted his attention from his own personal desire to be promoted to the happiness and success of his employees. He transferred his mindset to include empathy for others. As he rolled up his sleeves and communicated with compassion, he began to get to the heart of the matter. As he worked to repair and rebuild his team, he ultimately found himself personally renewed.

When we reflect on the chain of events that took place in this example, nothing happened within the manager's own actions except his experience of thought. He shifted his emphasis from himself to others, and, in the process, the angst around his own promotion dissolved. Once he shifted his priorities from self based to team based, the manager was awarded the promotion that he wanted all along.

Obsession with an outcome or "Shempa Logic" is quite different from setting a goal. Healthy organizations need goals to establish their projections and benchmarks for success. Annual business plans that include updated goals provide leaders with a target for immediate accomplishment and are fundamental to the structure that a company needs to thrive.

The problems occur when the goals become the basis for survival itself and the organization begins to lose flexibility and pliability. As the company's leaders harden around their goals, they begin to lose the wide view needed to move with the marketplace and the world.

This hardening or tightening develops a closed mind and heart. We become fixed on our thoughts of the outcome and before we know it, our thoughts own us. They become our tools of obsession that actually

Mindful Awareness
EXERCISE 12

Consider the following questions in order to lay the ground for successful improvements or the restructuring of your business:

- What might motivate and inspire me and my organization to be the best that we can be?
- Intuitively, what activities do not contribute to our success? Where is the connection between Right Intention and Right Action getting blocked?
- How can we begin to act in accord with the essential purpose of this business?

block our access to clarity of mind. By staying fixed and attached to an outcome, we become caught in the undertow of compulsion.

The good news is that the undertow is not fatal. In fact, the positive aspect of this undertow is what we can do with it. By becoming aware of and acknowledging our attachment or Shempa, we actually use the undertow to surface with fresh resilience. We do this by consciously letting go of the attachment to our fixated thoughts and looking at ourselves and our company with a new perspective. We can then regain our peripheral vision.

SURRENDER TO RESTRUCTURE

"We surrender because we would like to communicate with the world as it is."
—*Chogyam Trungpa Rinpoche,* Cutting Through Spiritual Materialism

In order to establish or fine-tune the accountability within your organization, you may find it is essential to surrender old practices and styles that no longer serve you. Establishing new methods and implementing new practices in the workplace will involve a willingness to restructure how you currently do business. This restructuring may be minor, or an entire restoration, depending on the current state of the business.

In the process of restructuring, we must peel away each layer of our organization until we hit the very essence of what moves and motivates us, our employees, and the market. We go to the root of our organizations, beyond the products and the profits, to look for the healthy assumptions, as well as the flaws. Restructuring includes asking difficult questions.

Only when we know the true, basic motivation of our organizations can we mindfully seek ways to restructure and improve their long-term performance through action. Equally interesting is the link that often is exposed with this exercise. You may find that the bottom-line inspiration of your organization is the same thing that motivates you as an executive. There is little separation between ourselves and our companies!

NO PAIN, NO GAIN

It can be argued that the concept of "no pain, no gain" originated with the Buddha. In order to restructure, we must be open to the reality of change. Often, with that change comes pain and sacrifice or, as the Buddha termed it, suffering.

However, the suffering is good news! The process of suffering allows for old patterns that are no longer effective to be gently broken down as you clear the path to cultivate a stronger foundation that is fertile with value-based principles, virtuous ethics, and quality work practices.

In Buddhist thinking, an action that brings only temporary pleasure can also be associated with suffering, as the gain is subject to an ending. It is this ending, this sense of finality, that creates the feeling of loss and ultimately leads to our suffering. Since the suffering arises from attachment or craving, it would stand to reason that it can also be overcome by the relaxing of that desire. When we let go of our intense desires to win or to be right, we can begin to open up and create the spacious mindset required to restructure our workplaces.

The process of restructuring goes beyond simply declaring a desire for change. Once you have begun the introspective journey of waking up your organization, the transformation will include a bit of pain before you reap the greatest gain.

It requires an acknowledgment that focusing solely on increased profits and net returns is simply not enough to evolve an organization in the long term. This management evolution requires a shedding of cravings for pure financial growth and a return to the basic concept of experiencing success by providing values-based leadership, authentic commitment, effective service, and quality products.

Leaders who choose to look beyond short-term win and immediate rewards are keenly positioned to wake up their organizations by learning from suffering and taking the steps required to recapture and reenact the soul of their organizations.

RIGHT ACTION: A WORK IN PROGRESS

The term "work in progress" is universally understood in businesses. The expression suggests the connection between action and growth, that a company is taking action to move itself forward. Because an organization's goals are always changing, its work is always in progress. Work is an evolution that has no end. There is always the next project, development, or discovery. This is true with our lives. We are all works in progress, constantly changing, growing, and upgrading ourselves and our lives in pursuit of a perfection that will never be obtained.

By accepting the reality that we will always be in works in progress, we can accept ourselves and our stumbles and transgressions in our journeys and continue to move forward with optimism. In the process, we also have the insight that can help to wake up our organizations.

This insight also takes us to a new level of growth, and it awakens the wisdom that tells us that the progress that we have made is irrelevant to the work itself. Whether we are excavating our paths and starting anew or polishing our efforts, our job is always about how we handle the process.

RIGHT LIVELIHOOD

> "My miraculous power and spiritual activity: Drawing water and chopping wood."
> —Layman P'ang

RIGHT LIVELIHOOD

Right Livelihood emphasizes loving what you do and working hard to help others build an enlightened life. The Buddha's principle of Right Livelihood does not reject the materialism of our corporate system but rather works within it to achieve abundance. Companies are in business to offer a service. This concept of service (or any work benefiting a customer) is part of the vision of Right Livelihood. Since our lives, and our occupations, are "works in progress," the Buddha's emphasis is less on what particular job one does and more concerned with how our success makes the world a better place.

There are everyday Buddhas in boardrooms across America who work tirelessly to make an impact in their companys and for their customers. Their leadership roles demand that they possess a passion for their work and are motivated by the unmitigated belief that they can contribute something positive to the world.

People who embrace a *Buddha: 9 to 5* discipline love going to work and show enthusiasm for every meeting, client, and employee connection. They look forward to rolling up their sleeves to bring a product or service to the attention of people who will benefit from it. Their passion and dedication to their work is a commitment that makes their companies or departments fun, dynamic places to be.

When framed by Right Livelihood, work means more than earning a paycheck. You are wide awake, achieving your aspirations and goals while injecting purpose into your life and the lives of others.

BUDDHA AND RIGHT LIVELIHOOD

The story of the Buddha offers us an example of Right Livelihood. The Buddha was not a religious leader or spiritual figure but rather an exceptional man who had the good fortune to be born into royalty. Yet, living in a vast and abundant circumstance was not enough for the young prince.

The story tells us that, disenchanted with his royal life as the heir to the throne of the kingdom of Sakyas, the young Buddha—then known as Prince Siddhartha Gautama—left his prosperous life at the royal palace and entered a life of poverty and simplicity.

When the young Buddha slipped out of the palace, he saw births, old age, sickness, and death. A compassion arose in Siddhartha that eventually encouraged him to leave his materialistic pleasures behind. Without him knowing that it was so, the Buddha was turning away from his old life too, and in the process, was practicing values-based leadership.

The Buddha made a "career change" of sorts that required the same courage and commitment to integrity that ordinary businesspeople experience today. This is a career change that can happen inwardly, in a shifting of priorities, or it can happen externally as you seek to find circumstances that are more closely aligned with your intentions.

The Buddha's story of inward transformation has its real-life version in countless companies around the world as they eschew short-term profit and questionable ethics to become more values-based and "awake."

When we have good jobs, with stable or even high levels of income, it is easy to get caught up in the pursuit of material pleasure. But when we discover that people suffer endlessly, compassion arises in us, and we become more aware of a higher purpose. We want to find a way to ease that suffering, thus we use our occupations and our businesses to reach out and benefit clients or customers. Through our products or services, we seek to make their lives easier, more prosperous, and more enlightened. We make our work environment enjoyable and creative and let people know that their talents are noticed and appreciated. Maintaining this awareness of suffering, and the desire to ease it, is a key to the motivation of being a Buddha in the workplace or the boardroom.

LOSING THE PASSION

Whether you own a start-up organization and take the big step to hire your first employees or expand your work force globally, the perseverance and level of commitment essential to success is the same. With each new hire, you add worth to the lives of others and contribute to their personal development. Your dedication, focus, and instincts help lay the foundation and set the groundwork for value-based growth—individually and as a company.

On the other hand, when we lose our love for what we do, the energy shifts and our assiduousness for Right Livelihood weakens. We are no longer connected to our Buddha nature, and we forget that our careers are choices.

Regardless of the level of seniority, many executives find themselves staying at jobs to attain a new title or a sabbatical or mark time as they yearn for their ultimate retirement. They sell out to the "golden handcuffs," which chain them to their jobs, while precious months and years fly aimlessly by.

Consider the saga of a close friend of mine who worked for twenty-five years for one of the most powerful trade associations in the United States. Ted had one of the most envied jobs in the industry. As a highly paid executive in the association market, his position had first-class benefits that at times stifled his occasional desire to make a career change.

Yet, as the years went by, Ted continued to lose his spark and no longer loved his work. As I watched him mark off the years toward his

Mindful Awareness
EXERCISE 13

Reflect on theses questions to help gauge if you are on the path to Right Livelihood:

- How do you spend your day at work? Are there areas in which you passively mark time?
- Can you remotivate yourself and recapture the enlightened spark for that aspect of your job?
- If not, can you delegate these responsibilities and fill the time with a task that is more meaningful to you?
- Are you able to create the same values in your workplace that you wish to create in your life?
- What are some simple first steps you can establish at work in order to create a workplace with a Buddha mindset?

quest for retirement, his bottom line shifted from appreciating his accomplishments to being more concerned with the net value of his pension plan.

Ted could have changed the course of his career by reconnecting with Right Livelihood and once again engaging while at work. He could have also made a job change to something more motivating, as several opportunities were presented to him over the course of his career. Or he simply could have changed his mindset about his position and had fun with it again.

Unfortunately, Ted's unhappy career path is a common and yet sad outcome of what happens to executives when they do not consider if they are engaging in Right Livelihood.

RIGHT LIVELIHOOD: THE GATEWAY TO FREEDOM

How do we know if we are engaged in Right Livelihood or if our work lives are narcissistic and self-absorbed? By shifting the focus from yourself to others you can access instant clarity to this question. By choosing to relax your preoccupation with yourself and the personal rewards long enough to rest in the spontaneity of the moment, you create a shift in consciousness that is very healthy. You free yourself from the quest for perfection knowing that it is not attainable.

Instead, you begin to trust again in your genuine capacity to think about others. This long overdue step toward happiness frees you from the burden of concern of your image and position. You taste the success of the moment rather than an overriding concern for your paycheck and retirement, and it feels good.

Jeff, head of a Buddhist retreat center, tasted this success first-hand. Formerly a successful entrepreneur in the high-tech industry, Jeff is gifted with the ability to cultivate dynamic organizations that make a difference in the world. He also is a seasoned meditator and understands the meaning of karma and the importance of helping the world through his work. At the peak of his career in the technology industry, Jeff made a decision to accept a position to build a meditation center in Northern Colorado.

The colossal challenge involved raising capital and then building the center that included the largest monument for peace in North America, in the form of a stupa. Jeff's vision included developing an infrastructure to support the monument so that the world could enjoy it. Jeff was passionate about building this infrastructure, which included a lodge, conference facility, and other buildings. The effort took seven years, and Jeff worked tirelessly, receiving a fraction of the pay he had in his former job.

Today, the complex, known as the Shambhala Mountain Center, is a spiritual retreat center and meeting place for thousands of individuals to visit and access their own inner serenity. Jeff's tireless perseverance and genuine belief that he was doing something to improve the world demonstrates the essence of Right Livelihood. By doing what he loved and shifting the emphasis from himself to others, Jeff entered the gateway to career freedom.

THE FREEDOM OF HONESTY

We embrace Right Livelihood by reinforcing our actions with a stronger work ethic. As our integrity becomes ingrained into our experience of Right Livelihood, we act with decency and truth. Each time we communicate from a place of honesty, it gets easier, and the productivity is greater. The evolution requires a certain amount of letting go—letting go of ego and of race against time itself. Instead, we open to the possibility of taking a leap of faith into the present moment.

A CASE STUDY OF POOR LIVELIHOOD

In the mid to late 1990s, women's health had become a major issue in the pharmaceutical industry, primarily due to the enormous market potential.

Fortune 100 pharmaceutical companies were racing each other to discover blockbuster remedies for menopause, depression, and osteoporosis. Breakthrough medical findings were offering new health options for women in their forties, fifties, and sixties, and the potential for growth of this industry segment was huge.

Mindful Awareness
EXERCISE 14

How have you taken a leap of faith in the context of your career and livelihood? The following exercises can help you define your success along the path of Right Livelihood:

- Identify instances when you have been concerned with your personal bottom line more than that of the company. What were the long-term results?

- Describe your Right Livelihood. On what values do you put your emphasis?

- How can you tap into your inner strength in order to make an impact that will carry forward in your life? What can you change to sharpen your own sense of integrity?

- Think of your long-term goals for Right Livelihood, both personally and for your company. Now think of what needs to be done to get there. Now, contemplate your present situation with these goals in mind. Can you project a successful career outcome by connecting with your long-term goals?

- Think of your life as a boat on the ocean. What is your current direction? Do you need to adjust to address the condition of the waves? How is the weather—the overall atmosphere and feeling?

- Finally, with these elements in mind, does anything need to change?

Leaders of the companies who were at the forefront of the race to capture this market were quick to take the credit for increased profits. Yet most of the same leaders were men and incapable of truly identifying with the end user of their products, menopausal women.

The majority of the youthful managers charged with marketing the products simply looked at the numbers and financial results of the drugs, with little empathy for the case studies and patients who would ultimately experience the breakthroughs.

I experienced this painful reality firsthand. One of our clients was a major pharmaceutical company, and we were hired to launch their predicted blockbuster osteoporoses product that was comarketed with their leading antidepression drug. Corporate pressures continually placed the drug's product managers in compromising positions. Daily they were forced to choose between increasing the pace of the product's performance in the marketplace and preserving their own integrity. This compromise involved choosing between delivering assumptions about their products' potential rather than marketing the true benefits of their drugs.

At the annual meeting for 2,500 sales representatives who were there marketing a blockbuster antidepressant, management made the conscious decision to select short-term success over Right Livelihood.

The patent for the company's leading antidepressant would soon expire, and the company was scrambling for a new use of the product and FDA indication. Having exhausted all other markets, their strategy was to target the pediatric segment. Having worked for months on end on this launch, I sat in the audience, seven months pregnant, and realized that our clients were not motivated by their desire to free their patients of depression, but to keep their shareholders happy. While in some cases antidepression medication may be necessary, children's health statistics show that far more prescriptions for antidepressants are written than actually needed.

Management sent their sales force to aggressively market the product to pediatric offices across the nation, touting their assumed benefits. By promising a "cure" to parents with challenging children, these companies and their management teams placed their jobs and bottom line ahead of Right Livelihood.

When we exercise Right Livelihood, we understand that the real bottom line is found in those individuals who can step up to the challenge and preserve their own integrity by aligning with what is in the best interest of those whose lives their products and services affect.

A CASE STUDY OF RIGHT LIVELIHOOD

Emotions and impassioned pleas are given little weight in the executive committees of most major corporations today. Yet, one of our clients, who was the senior vice president of women's health care for a major pharmaceutical company, was an example of leading to Right Livelihood, despite the consequences. Mary Ann was passionate about her job and the products she was charged with delivering to the marketplace.

She reported to a chairman, president, and executive committee who were driven solely by the bottom line. This group of leaders put the stockholders interests first, and they saw Mary Ann's emotional attachment to her work as a conflict of interest. Their priorities were about the speed with which they brought drugs to market and delivery of the right numbers to Wall Street.

Mary Ann's commitment to hold to her convictions demonstrated the essence of awake leadership. At the launch meeting, she explained the benefits of a hormone replacement therapy drug designed to fight

Mindful Awareness
EXERCISE 15

Take a few minutes to sit quietly and breathe before answering these tough questions!

Consider a time when you were placed in the position of compromising your gut instincts in order to improve results.

- What were the long- versus short-term results of those actions?
- What would you do differently today?

osteoporosis with firsthand experience and compassion. She let go of her concerns about the president of the corporation's judgment and spoke from the heart. During this presentation to more than 2,500 sales reps, Mary Ann delivered a message of the heart, one that touched her audience as she unrolled the product's authentic bottom-line benefits.

The speech broke the mold. Most drug launch presentations are filled with statistics and show staged testimonials by actors portraying patients. Mary Ann's story was about her mother's fight against osteoporosis, which she lost. Shortly after the launch, Mary Ann resigned under pressure, but she paved the way for true leaders in the health care industry to speak from the heart, guided by their own convictions.

Her allegiance to Right Livelihood ultimately paid off personally as well. Mary Ann went on to lead the way for an even larger pharmaceutical company that recognized her gifts as a true leader in marketing medicine.

FOR RIGHT LIVELIHOOD, BE THE BEE

Aerodynamically, the bumblebee should not be able to fly, as its wings are too small to support its body. But the bee does not know this, so it flies anyway. When my partner and I launched CEM in 1988, a friend gave me a wall plaque that said, "Be the Bee."

The total net worth of the company at inception was two telephones, two skirted convention tables that served as desks, and one computer that my partner and I shared. We spent all of our "capital" on business cards and letterheads.

Who would have predicted that the business would have grown to a $10 million agency in twelve years?

It seemed like the odds were against us and we should not succeed, especially when our former employer tried to put us out of business. But we were so spellbound by the energy of creating a business that we loved that we ignored signs of potential failure. With relentless commitment and belief, we forged ahead, and the business grew.

Call after call, pitch after pitch, we slowly earned the confidence of dozens of *Fortune* 500 clients. By staying in the "zone" of Right Livelihood, loving what we were doing, and doing good work, we began to cultivate a thriving business. The emphasis was on others and staying in the moment, spontaneous as possible to deliver exciting work.

Our true power was within ourselves. We had the desire to build a business, and the belief—some would call it naivety—to know that we could. Fueled by our desires and beliefs, we immersed ourselves in the present moment to deliver cutting-edge creativity. Whenever we felt obstacles of fear or self-doubt begin to arise, we would come back to our fearless Buddha nature and desire to make an impact. We were motivated by a passion to always deliver the perfect creative solution for our clients. Before we made our first sale, we had already become successful. We were not obsessed with the future or racing against time. We were living the gift of staying present and loving what we do. We were "being the bees."

AT THE TIP OF THE NEEDLE

How did you get to where you are today? Was your career path strategic or was there an accomplishment early in your profession that set the course for your success? Did you tenaciously climb your way to

Mindful Awareness
EXERCISE 16

Reflect back on the early stages of your career when you were "the bee."

- What aspects of your current position will improve by staying in the present, free of attachment?
- What would you do to increase market share if there were no stakes involved?
- How would you choose to impact the world through your position if your only concern was social responsibility?

this point in time, single-minded and focused on landing your current position? Or was the path more gradual or serendipitous?

Few people have had the fortunate karma to direct their career path with flawless predictability. While many of today's executives have positioned themselves for success, an equal number of CEOs fell into their first jobs through unforeseen circumstances.

Some of us have chosen such a fast pace that our career tracks resemble a highway with frequent lane changes and accelerated moves. Along with this pace comes sudden stops to avoid collisions. It is during these times that we are graced with the brief but essential opportunity to slow down and go within.

By slowing down long enough to evaluate the vastness of our influence—the impact that we make on the lives of others and the world— we are suddenly faced with our accountability. We know that we have the power to inspire and motivate, or to persuade and manipulate. The choice is ours.

Whether your career path was methodically planned or extemporized and spontaneous, where you have landed is not coincidental. Your karmic path has delivered to you this privileged opportunity to make day-to-day decisions that will impact the lives of others and therefore impact the world.

As the Buddha at work, your choice for Right Livelihood provides you with the noble distinction to make decisions that are threaded with both accountability and compassion; decisions that are equitable and acute; decisions that deliver maximum results and yet at the same time are discriminating and come from the heart.

In a word, you must learn how to be reasonable with your employees and suppliers without compromising your standards.

How do we sharpen our accountability and still be reasonable? How do we finesse this dance to deliver balance and harmony while in the pressure of difficult times? With P&L goals and boardroom pressures, employee expectations and stockholder demands, how do we stay reasonable?

We stay reasonable by realizing that our happiness and the happiness of others are not two different things. We remember that all human beings experience pain, fear, and sadness. Simply, we all experience life and death.

By contemplating the notion of death, we take ourselves to the tip of the needle. We ask ourselves the difficult questions. What do we want to accomplish before we die? What do we want to be remembered for? What legacy can we leave behind in this lifetime?

By acknowledging the sudden reality that your life and brilliant career will eventually come to an end, you can create the compelling gap needed in your mind and heart to make reasonable decisions. In this knowledge, you begin to lean into your hard choices and take your life to the tip of the needle.

TIMBERLAND

For Jeffrey Swartz, the path was chosen. However, how he paved it is a different story altogether:

Jeffrey Swartz is on a mission to help stomp out illiteracy and poverty in the world with his innovative company, Timberland. Built on hard work and a solid "do good and do well" philosophy, the third generation owner of the family-led public company represents the soul of Right Livelihood.

Nathan Swartz began his boot-making company in the 1920s. In 1973, the brand name Timberland was born to market the innovative and functional waterproof boot, still indigenous to work and construction sites across America today. In the past twenty-five years, the brand expanded to include casual shoes and apparel for men, women, and children.

But the business's emphasis is on more than just retail. CEO and President Jeffrey Swartz is proud that his company is different from other traditional shareholder-driven organizations. The $1.5 billion corporation spends a large part of its assets on programs that are community driven. It's highly recognized "Path of Service" program gives each of its 4,300 employees forty hours of paid off time annually to volunteer for a community service. Timberland also offers a six-month sabbatical to employees who desire to pursue a personal dream if it benefits the community.

Ironically, Swartz's emphasis on giving back has paid off well for Timberland's shareholders, out-performing the S&P 500 and NASDAQ, and leading its industry for ten years. Boasting a 10.1 percent profit margin in 2005, Swartz has managed to successfully finesse the obligations to both shareholders and corporate social responsibility.

In 2006, Timberland led numerous environmental initiatives to "Make It Better," including introducing environmentally friendly packaging and enforcing "green" store building and renovation standards with the use of recycled materials. The company also launched a solar array—a system that will generate 60 percent of its own power at a large Timberland distribution plant in California, the first corporate project of its kind in the region—at the company's Earth Day celebration.

First in waterproof boots, first in the use of solar technology—who says that Right Livelihood cannot improve the bottom line?

Once you have accessed your own tenderness, the option to turn back and operate from a cutthroat bottom-line mindset is no longer available. Once you are on the top of the needle, committed to practicing Right Livelihood, you have nowhere to go. You are exposed and present. Taking care of others and the world is now the only choice!

Staff Path Practice

As a manager, one of your most delicate and yet vital jobs is to ensure that each of your employees is in a position that is a good fit for his or her and the organization. Employees are not motivated solely by their paychecks or their titles; they want to know that they are making a difference. Use this model to help your staff realize their own significance:

Strategic: Shift the focus at a meeting from short-term to long-term potential. Lay the groundwork for how their efforts are affecting their future and the future of others in the department.

Tactical: Ask direct questions that trigger a connection with the job that they are doing and their appreciation for it. Whose lives are you impacting with your performance? How can you accelerate and improve your importance? If you could change your livelihood, would you, and if so, to what? (Be prepared: These are gutsy questions that could provoke change in your staffing. However, the change in the long term will be positive, as you will be building a stronger organization as a result of that change.)

Operational: Perhaps your team is committed to their jobs, but they would like time to explore personal interests. How can you as a group free up time to allow for individuals to pursue their Right Livelihood? Evaluate how you spend your time and appreciate the talents of your team.

When a developer walks away from a real estate transaction that promises a 32 percent return because it will displace the homes of hundreds of people, or a national business magazine publishes an article that is detrimental to one of its top advertisers, the path of Right Livelihood has met its edge.

The good news that comes with the principle of Right Livelihood is that you can also relax a bit. By appreciating your talents, ability, and fortunate circumstance, you realize that you are destined on some level to work hard and that work will help the world. There is relief in that knowledge. Because you can no longer compromise your authentic bottom line, your decisions become much easier to make.

RIGHT EFFORT

> "The big secret in life is that there is no big secret. Whatever your goal, you can get there if you're willing to work."
> —Oprah Winfrey

RIGHT EFFORT

The classic Buddhist analogy of Right Effort usually depicts the slow but graceful and determined walk of an elephant. The elephant has strength, dignity, and perseverance. As the elephant walks along focused on the ground in front of her, she employs her peripheral vision to capture the world with spontaneous pleasure, yet all the while has a great impact on her surroundings. Just like many of America's great enterprises, elephants possess the grace and sure-footed wisdom to make great things happen with what appears to be little effort. That is because those companies stay true to their mission and vision to get their work done.

Elephant-like corporations such as IBM, Hewlett-Packard, and American Express keep their feet planted firmly on the ground while simultaneously examining the marketplace with panoramic precision. They know where they are going and are unstoppable in their quest for greatness. Their gentle but tough work ethic epitomizes Right Effort.

The concept of Right Effort in the workplace typically evokes images of strength, hard work, and exertion to obtain a goal. We know what it is that we have to do, and we roll up our sleeves and struggle to get the job done. This conventional style of effort is masculine by nature and represents the blood, sweat, and tears approach that dominated the old corporate American work paradigm. This model may have served the workforce well in the Industrial Age, but in today's hi-tech, hi-touch climate it is not as effective as it once was. *Buddha: 9 to 5* presents an opportunity to try a gentler, wiser, and more intelligent style of engaging Right Effort.

In order to maximize your potential and the results of your efforts, you must approach your job with a sharper, smarter mindset. By combining your intellect and intuition, you can evoke the Right Effort required to lead your company to greatness without having to shake the trees and only reach the low hanging fruit. By implementing Right Speech, Right Action, and Right Intention, you are positioned to accomplish a great deal with what is seemingly less effort.

Right Effort is not suggesting that you must work to exhaustion to succeed. Rather, the path implies an opposite approach. With Right Effort, we realize that creating a successful and balanced life is possible. You use wisdom, experience, and confidence to cut through old work habits and perform at the top of your game. Right Effort is the path that cultivates our efficiency to live and work in balance.

How do you change old patterns of communication and management styles that no longer serve you in order to take your efforts to a new level of efficiency and productivity? The *Buddha: 9 to 5* approach offers the tools for change with the instruction to turn your efforts both inward and outward. By creating the space inside yourself and your organization for introspection, you can access the issues that block growth. Going beneath the surface while maintaining a long-term view of your business offers you the greatest potential to create change within the leadership of your organization.

The process of continually going inward through meditation, introspection, and contemplation jump-starts your passion to ignite the external change that will benefit you, your employees, and your customers. Right Effort is the expression of the interdependence of inward and outward change occurring simultaneously.

Right Effort requires patience. The drive-through, get-the-job-done, task-oriented mentality present in boardrooms and executive offices across corporate America is simply no longer effective or intelligent.

Right Effort involves taking the time to slow down just long enough to go inward in order to reveal the wisdom needed to create the outward change. This step is not intended to lose momentum or impede productivity, but rather through conscious introspection, the yield for success can increase. The social progressive giving program of Ben and Jerry's, for example, depicts the type of grassroots efforts that can change a community when a company looks inward to realize its possibility. The leadership of this socially conscious ice cream business emphasizes Right Effort through its commitment to donate to environmental and social causes.

These acts of introspection and taking action on the findings are not easy for many people. It can be a difficult decision to give away

Mindful Awareness
EXERCISE 17

Evaluate the current efforts within your organization:

- What are the ways in which my organization can benefit from Right Effort?
- In what ways do we overextend, exhaust, or strain ourselves to accomplish our goals? Does this hurt morale?
- Imagine your organization operating in a fluid, effortless way. What needs to change about the present state of your company in order for it to operate like this?
- What can you change about the way you personally conduct business?

hard-earned profits to charities or do the right thing if it means the possibility of a smaller profit margin. The good news is that opportunities to expand your prosperity are always available to you. Your wisdom and Right Effort are your tools to that abundance. However, you must make a conscious decision to use them.

RIGHT EFFORT BEGINS WITHIN

The Buddha offered us Four Great Efforts that can assist us in looking inward in order to cultivate our own Right Effort. By examining these Four Efforts from the point of view of a Buddha in the workplace and in the boardroom, we are developing our own inner resources that will ultimately benefit our decision making and external activity.

Great Effort 1: The Effort to Avoid

This principle does not refer to avoidance in the traditional sense—such as the way we avoid situations or people that cause us pain. Rather, avoidance of this kind challenges us to evade that which is detrimental to our own hard work. Perhaps you are in a position that is privy to confidential information, including details on the performance of some of your peers. At a company gathering, a few colleagues begin to gossip about one of the employees that you have information about. The Effort to Avoid would be to not participate in this idle chatter, regardless of the temptation to socialize. By not contributing to the discussion, you have saved yourself much worry and guilt.

The effort to avoid can spare you much frustration and help change the way you habitually deal with your thoughts. Having simple awareness of your negative thoughts is the first step to avoiding detrimental or counterproductive tendencies in your work. Think, for example, of aspects of your job that trigger negative thoughts: a colleague or employee who pushes your buttons, a competitor who drives you to the edge of hostility, or a fear of not meeting an aggressive sales or profit goal.

We have the ability to catch these negative thoughts as they arise and relax around them enough to recognize their insubstantiality or better yet, convert them to positive solutions. Knowing that your mind can be tamed enough to control your thoughts brings power.

Great Effort 2: The Effort to Overcome

If we don't catch our negative thoughts in the avoidance stage, then they will build momentum. Consider how your level of frustration would escalate if you thought that an internal competitive situation was undermining your success. Perhaps you are attempting to introduce a new policy that encourages employees to be more environmentally responsible, but the COO views this cause as just an add-on to the bottom line. By taking this push-back from the COO personally, you can see how your desire to implement the change conflicts with the COO's conservative views. You might also predict that this conflict will snowball into a major internal conflict. Rather than working through this challenge with a clear head, you attack the COO and call him or her socially shallow and money driven. Your defense becomes a striking offense. Had you avoided this aggressive tactic, you may have had better success.

We do not want to face the possible failure or nonacceptance of our ideas, regardless of how genuine or socially responsible they may be. Our thoughts can consume us because we have created a reactive comfort zone that is set up to shield us from our insecurities and possible failure. It is easier to blame the boss or company policy for failed initiative rather than own our shortcomings. This method of "ready, fire, aim" management is not helpful.

As managers, we have all experienced times of frustration when we reacted to a challenge before thinking about the results. By making a concerted effort to overcome the habitual inner aggression that builds in times of frustration, we slow down momentum's highway long enough to regroup and assess what is really important. Overcoming our aggression at work, regardless of how subtle it is, is the first step to enlightened management.

Great Effort 3: The Effort to Develop

Developing the virtues that you want to maintain at work—such as patience, generosity, and compassion—serves you well and strengthens your overall performance. This effort is the result of the space you created by avoiding or overcoming negative thoughts. Thus, you now have plenty of room for thoughts that offer brighter results—whether it is in company morale or product development or wherever you focus your attention.

The effort to develop requires a mindful and precise approach to leadership. The development begins with making a deliberate effort to access and engage your virtues in a precise way on a daily basis. This effort may be as subtle as pausing to make kind eye contact with an employee or as intense as provoking a conversation that addresses work integrity and ethics. The Buddha refers to this effort as "practice in action."

Great Effort 4: The Effort to Maintain

When we become aware of the old negative patterns that no longer serve us at work, we can finally let them go and free our minds to focus on the qualities that we do want to develop. Thus your new personal mission is to preserve your mindful ability to access and engage those positive qualities that effectively promote healthy changes in your organization.

DUALISTIC THINKING

Often our thoughts are conflictive and have a double-edged quality. You say that you want to be more generous to your employees while the company slices away at their benefits package in order to strengthen its profitability. You want to show a colleague appreciation for a job well done, but his or her performance actually brings up a competitive aggression inside.

These conflictive thought patterns are known in Buddhism as dualistic thinking. They exist in everyone. In the Buddha's perspective, they give us something to work with, which is a good thing. By making the effort to evaluate your aggression or directly go to the root of your frustration, you can begin to work with your reactions to difficult circumstances. This is where the change actually begins. This work ultimately clarifies and opens the passage to refine our leadership qualities.

The Effort to Notice Dualistic Thoughts

Recall a time when you have obsessed on a thought. Perhaps you were fixated on the outcome of landing a major account, winning an internal argument, or contemplating a conflict with an employee. Have you noticed that if you try to stop the thought, you actually pay much more attention to it?

Pushing away your thoughts causes them to get larger and occupy more mind space. Attention on an idea, regardless of the nature of the thought, will expand it and give it more power over you. Once you begin to obsess on a concept, you can also see how easily dualistic thinking can develop.

On the other hand, by being aware of your thoughts as they are occurring, you can train yourself to sharpen your awakened mind and eliminate the confusion that arises with dualistic thinking. You strengthen your intelligence to make decisions with an inspired clarity.

THREE THOUGHTS, THREE ACTIONS TOWARD RIGHT EFFORT

There are three primary levels of obsession associated with negative thought and, respectively, three recommended approaches to dealing with such thoughts.

The first level involves negative thoughts that are in your mind on a minor or subtle level. These are the thoughts that most executives accept and deal with, given the reality that we all encounter some frustration in our daily workplace.

For example, you are scheduled for what is anticipated to be an unpleasant meeting with an employee, a meeting in which you will give critical feedback. As your day begins, your anxiety about the meeting arises. These thoughts have the potential to consume your morning and, yet, by being aware of your anxiety, you choose to put it aside until it is time to deal with the situation. You acknowledge the thought and let it go, knowing that you will eventually have the employee discussion firsthand and in the present.

The second form of thought, known as "hot thought," is a bit stickier. These levels of thoughts are so "hot" or intense that you cannot let them go and, in fact, they have the potential to totally occupy your mind. Yet, even though they are annoyingly present, you can still choose to ignore them and focus on your other tasks. When such thoughts arise, the best approach is to again acknowledge the thought, and then, tell yourself that the situation will eventually pass and that it is workable. Just the knowledge that it is workable provides the relief needed to avoid obsession.

For example, you are scheduled for an employee meeting, but this time it is for the purpose of terminating a person's job. The individual has worked for you for a long time, and you are emotionally attached to their happiness. However, you know that this decision is best for the organization and the employee.

On the day of the meeting, you cannot let go of your thoughts around this dreaded meeting and the emotional discomfort that will occur. However, you are still able to function by telling yourself that the situation, and thus, your thoughts, are workable. You can actually access brief relief and focus on other aspects of your job.

The third and most severe form of negative thought is neurotic obsession. This level of obsession has the potential to affect your immediate sanity. Essentially, a specific thought or series of thoughts around an issue keep you in such a spin that there is no stopping the thought.

This form of thought has also been termed "wild mind," and while it is the most intense, it offers the juiciest potential to learn from. When we are confronted with our wildly spinning minds, we are offered the opportunity to ride the wave of the situation in order to experience the ultimate relief and joy of the change that will occur. The process requires you to be aware and connected to the experience.

When we are aware of our neurosis, we can actually feel the emotion to such a degree that our creativity and ability to solve problems rises to the occasion. Level three provides no other choice than to stay focused on the thought until the obsession dissolves. The only relief is time and the knowledge that the situation and therefore the thought around it will eventually pass. We are not capable of immediate rebound in such a situation. Instead, we ride the wave with confident intensity that time will heal. We commit to doing this because we know that the end benefits are there.

In order to cultivate discriminating awareness, we need to be able to be aware of our emotions as they arise. The more intimately we know our own emotions and hot spots, the easier it will be to dilute their power and strengthen our virtues that lead to greater success. Doing this work is the essence of Right Effort and leads us to the joy of being in the moment and enmeshing ourselves in the sweet nectar of the direct experience.

RIGHT EFFORT LIES IN THE DIRECT EXPERIENCE

American Buddhist nun and meditation master Pema Chodron eloquently described the essence of being in the moment when she exclaimed: "Peace on Earth abides with our own direct experience."

Our business lives contain thousands of diversions. Our preoccupation with hitting financial and personal goals clogs our ability to be completely present. We struggle and fixate on our sense of duty. We miss out on the uplifted inspiration that resides in the moment. Our goals and accomplishments provide an outlet and a justifiable decoy that keeps us from accessing our direct experience. Essentially, we have mastered the ability to plan our way out of our direct experiences and, therefore, out of our lives.

Enormous responsibilities and lofty titles help to justify our inability to stay in a direct experience at work. We fill the hours with meetings, budget reviews, strategic planning, and routine tasks.

While most of these responsibilities are essential to the growth of an organization, the way we choose to engage in our jobs provides the groundwork for a personally enriching or impassive experience.

The objective of *Buddha: 9 to 5* is to infuse our goals and visions with an in-the-moment awareness, an immediate awakened presence. When we are absorbed in a direct experience, we feel open, honest, and powerful. The result is an expanded mind and a fresh alternative to how we think about our work.

The ability to access the direct experience is the fundamental key to Right Effort. You can use it to motivate yourself and your employees and therefore increase productivity. You are no longer inspired simply by a goal set by the company for increased production and profitability. Rather, you are intuitively compelled to taste success through the excitement and satisfaction that comes with delivering spontaneous Right Effort. Your bottom line becomes your ability to stay in the direct experience in order to produce good work.

BLOCKING THE DIRECT EXPERIENCE

The pressures of our jobs can work against us and keep us detached from our direct experiences. The continuous burden of problem solving and exposure to negative challenges intuitively draws our minds like a magnet to a place of resistance. We resist a client's demand for better service, an employee's cry for attention, or our board's request for increased profitability. As demands heighten, we seek space and relief from the pressures, and like caged birds sense that there is no way out.

Feeling our ego-based internal buttons being pushed, we seek shelter in the familiar tendency to tighten and close up. We deflect the judgments, demands, and criticism of others with sarcasm, denial, or aggression. We are steeped in defensiveness and pride and feel the need to protect our position, judge others, or in some cases even fight back or attack.

Ironically, when we ambush ourselves with fear or conflict, we are actually placing attention onto the negative feeling and inviting it in. It is at this point that our self-talk strategies kick in. These strategies are habitual ways of handling situations that we employ over and over again, whether they are effective or not. We ignore, manipulate, threaten, or blame, or we use whatever strategy feels familiar to our personality or style.

Along with the strategy come our defensiveness, emotions, and ego, which further block us from directly experiencing the challenge at hand. Essentially, we have paralyzed our ability to access our creativity, which could have been used to discover the best solution.

When we resist and fall out of a direct experience with our board members, clients, or colleagues, we have interrupted our ability to communicate. We have road blocked our access to the pure intention of our thoughts and disregarded our core values—the basis of our existence.

When times like these arise, what steps can we take to neutralize the situation in order to recover our balanced footing? How do we preserve and hold on to a direct experience? How can we catch the symptoms of wanting to shut down before they occur and consume the present moment? The first step is to engage your awareness and catch any dissension as it is occurring. Begin by backing up to notice

Mindful Awareness
EXERCISE 18

Choose a topic that you are preoccupied by at work.

Is that preoccupation preventing you from having a direct experience with your work and accomplishments? Now, allow yourself to return to your fixation on the issue, but this time try to change the intensity of the thoughts by placing less of a significance on them. Tell yourself that this is not that important; it is not life or death. Now, break the thought pattern again and do something very different. Direct your attention to the sky, an object, or another person. Think of anything but the subject of your obsession.

Now, think about your core values. How do they translate to the issue that you are contemplating? By focusing on your core values, have you accessed an instant of clarity and diluted the preoccupation or obsessive thoughts?

the potential conflict, that thorny rose bush that is in front of you, drawing you in.

Face to face with the conflict, you can choose to handle the tension in a new way, to do something different. You can resist the temptation to shut down or explode and instead, stay focused on exactly what is occurring in the moment.

By consciously staying immersed in the present moment, you have the opportunity to catch the angst or defensiveness as it comes up. You have clarity and the peripheral vision to evaluate the present condition and make decisions that are in the long-term, best interest of the company.

In order to recapture your mindfulness and values, you intently return to the moment by feeling it. You feel the compassion for others and yourself. You then consciously direct your efforts into a path of

Mindful Awareness
EXERCISE 19

Recall a business experience that had an Olympic level of competition, when the stakes were high and there was a limited window of opportunity to win.

- What ethics, if any, were compromised to ensure a win?
- How could you have raised the bar of ethics and implemented Right Effort and still have succeeded?

doing good work with Right Intention. It is only when you come back to the direct experience of the moment, come back to your desire to communicate from your true basic goodness that you can operate and manage with fluidity and kindness.

The direct experience, then, provides the ground for the Right Effort, enabling you to access your personal bottom line and lead from your core values.

THE RELIEF OF RIGHT EFFORT

The Buddha said that suffering has an alternating quality: Life is not intended to be lived in continuous pain, and yet, neither is life one long chorus line of joy and bliss. Rather, suffering alternates between good and bad, happy and sad. This blinking quality of suffering provides relief from pain and interrupts the loftiness of pleasure. It keeps us grounded and ready for the next round of lessons. This phenomenon is the relief that we receive from applying Right Effort in all circumstances.

When we experience fear, cutbacks, and failure, we are actually positioned to go to the next level by asking the honest question, "How is this workable?" As dharma leader Chogyam Trungpa Rinpoche said many times in his teachings, "It's all workable." Tough times are also the richest times. It is during our most difficult periods that we go within, analyze our habitual patterns of ego and control, and salvage what is workable. In essence, we are consciously working with our discomfort.

Staff Path Practice

If your business is facing challenging times, this is a great departmental tool to help your staff think outside of the box and integrate workable solutions:

Strategic: Identify as a group the primary challenge at hand and discuss specifically how it is affecting the company's ability to reach its goal. Are revenues down due to market conditions or is the competition showing more exertion? Are your systems and procedures slowing, clogging the productivity and hampering your ability to get the work done? Really dig deep into the issue with honest, objective evaluations.

Tactical: Next brainstorm solutions. Write them down even if they seem unrealistic. Often a strong idea can stem from a crazy idea. Begin by identifying the desired outcome and then work back into the situation to target where you are getting stuck. Highlight areas that are blocking the growth.

Operational: Establish action steps that tackle the specific issues identified in the two steps above. Stay focused and do not get too far in front of yourself. Remember, in working with Right Effort, the primary lesson is that it is all workable.

As we let go of the deception of our ten minutes, ten months, or ten years of fame and wealth, we suddenly see with new eyes how stuck we really are. We realize that pleasure without doing the work is hollow and short lived. It is at this point of introspection, this epiphany of truth, that we go deep within and find the courage to acknowledge that it is all workable and that we are indeed ready to apply Right Effort.

RIGHT MINDFULNESS

"The mind's nature is intrinsically pure."
—The Buddha

RIGHT MINDFULNESS

The Buddha believed that the mind is by nature genuine and luminous. It is the unrestrained, incandescent qualities of the mind that expand our creativity and give us the mental space to experience reality. We experience the moment from a wide-angle lens and engage in a way that has big vision for our companies and ourselves.

This spacious awareness provides the confidence to trust our own thoughts and the outcome of our actions. In essence, we expand our view to encompass more than just our own personal dilemmas. We extend out to others and include their well-being in our choices and decisions.

Climb into your mind and have a look. What motivates you? Is it money, power, a sense of purpose? Do you resonate with the thought of making a difference in your organization, in society, in the world? As you honestly examine your motives, you may like certain aspects of what you see and feel good about yourself. You may also see the harshness and critical qualities of some of your thoughts and come face to face with your own agitations. More than likely you will uncover a bit of both mindsets and taste the bittersweet residue of your intrinsically good but compromised mind.

By stepping back to scrutinize what triggers and controls your thoughts, you also are examining your bottom line. It is this examination and introspection that ignites the process of waking up. It will keep you focused on your view, the very foundation of change.

RIGHT MINDFULNESS AND VIEW UNDER PRESSURE

Even the highest-paid, respected executives in corporate America occasionally lose sight of their view. As managers under pressure, we will experience events that cloud our clarity and distort composure. A boss or board member may challenge your opinion or position, the market may turn and threaten your financial security, or you may be stressed by a critical deadline.

In these various instances, when you are experiencing the pressure of your job, you also have the opportunity to experience Right

Mindfulness. Ironically, it happens that our insecurities, tribulations, and uncomfortable moments offer us the best workable material. When we directly face our fears and frustrations, we are weaving the rare and intricate fabric used to design the rich tapestry of our authentic selves.

By training the mind and embracing challenges as opportunities to wake up, we develop the skillfulness to hold to our view. We remove the lamination that temporarily shields us from the discomfort of the moment. Strengthening our ability to fully experience each moment forms a keyhole for the world to shine directly into our tender heart. Once open, we have an unlimited view of our potential and the impact we are destined to make on the world.

Unfortunately for most of us, the human experience provides for both the freedom of unencumbered mindfulness and a tightened, self-interested alternative. We want a certain result, but we place our energy in the opposite direction. By applying Right Mindfulness, we can alleviate this dualistic thinking.

CALMING THE MIND TO STOP THE SPINOUT

The practice of calming the mind on a daily basis provides clarity and inner peace. When we relax and become still, we are able to experience the present with tender simplicity. We release all judgment, worry, and fear, and we activate kindness. We simply *are*.

The pressures of our jobs can make calming the mind a challenge. The constant chatter in our minds, even though it goes unnoticed much of the time, is a part of our minute-by-minute existence. The more we obsess over our self-absorbed thoughts, the less spontaneous and in touch with the moment we become. We dull our own potential to access our inherent richness and block our ability to make a difference. As discussed in Path 6: Right Effort, when we fixate on thought, we usually enter an intellectual race to nowhere.

Our thoughts have no clear destiny; they are loose, out of control and perpetual.

This mental spinout can occur at anytime and anywhere. You could be in the shower on a Monday morning preparing to go to work and before you have even towel dried, it is 3:00 P.M. in your mind. You could be on the subway on the way to meet with a board member, but in your mind, you have already completed the conversation. Our rehearsed, controlled thoughts disable our ability to listen and access the true two-way communication that is optimum for a successful meeting.

As mentioned, we are always engaged in thought. Whether you are in the car driving to a client presentation or dining out with your spouse to unwind from the intensity of the day, your mind is thinking.

When you channel this energy around making the deal, winning the business, or beating the competition, you lay the groundwork to achieving that goal.

On the other hand, if you do not exercise the discipline to train your mind, you set yourself up for spinning out with your thoughts. Before you know it, your mind is randomly moving from thought to thought. It is this erratic mindset that actually prevents you from achieving your goal.

What this boils down to is that our own neurosis dilutes the uniqueness of the moment. We cripple our ability to transcend the obsession. We, in effect, stifle our true potential.

But what if we don't actually win the business or make the deal? Is our life affected fatally? Or are we actually being handed the gift of alternative thinking? Is this an opportunity to use our mind to cultivate a solution that is more fulfilling and prosperous? By letting go of the desire or result that we so tightly cling to, we can make space for the possibility of a fresh approach, a new and more exciting journey.

When we train the mind to be present, we slow down the speediness and open our creativity. There are several ways to access this wisdom. Training in meditation is one technique that is described in the next chapter, Path 8: Right Concentration. You can also mentally block off several brief moments of each day to consciously notice your thoughts. Do this during idle times when your mind has the opportunity to wander the most, such as during your commute, in an elevator, or in the shower. You may even write your random thoughts down. Do this exercise without judgment of the thoughts themselves, but simply as an exercise to sharpen your awareness of what is going on in your mind.

Appreciation is another way to tap into the moment. Make it a point to appreciate specific aspects of the day that would otherwise go unnoticed. The smell of the rain, a phone call from a close friend whom you have not connected with in a while, the laughter of children in a park nearby, the afterglow of a sunset. Appreciation brings you right to the heart of the present moment and provides relief from your racing thoughts.

In-the-moment training actually provides the spaciousness needed to make decisions that are far more reaching and effective—decisions that are made from a deeper awareness. With that awareness comes an appreciation for what is truly important. We know when we are fixating on a certain point and when we are letting go. We base our decisions upon long-term results that are interdependent with others. Manipulation of our thoughts is no longer necessary, because we rest in the true nature of our mind and make decisions from Right View and Right Intention.

Is it possible that this discovery can spring from sitting on the edge of your chair or bed for ten minutes each morning before you open the flood gates of mental obsession?

The only answer is to try it for yourself.

Mindful Awareness
EXERCISE 20

Think of a specific obstacle at work that you are currently experiencing. Focus only on the qualities and conditions of the situation rather than seeking an outcome. Each time your mind wanders to your desired outcome, go back to simply being with the situation.

- Examine the qualities of what comes up for you about the situation by staying with it. Is it intense or dull? Does it bring up anxiety or are you content with the situation as it is in this moment?
- Now, for a split second completely shift your thoughts from this situation to something completely unrelated like the sound of the wind through a tree or the cool sensation of plunging into the ocean.
- Return to your thoughts of the work situation. Did you open up a bit of space to look at the situation in a different light, if only for a split second? Can you release the anxiety associated with the situation? Does it feel workable?

This exercise allows for your wisdom to rise to the surface. The more you train the mind to concentrate without condition, the more prolific you will become at accessing your wisdom.

CHAOS IN THE BOARDROOM

Chaos is the opposite of a quiet mind. It stirs up unwanted energy, stimulates defensive thought, and creates a provocative attraction to conflict. We might assume that conflict is part of being a leader. Although this may occasionally be true, more frequently disparity and discord in the workplace translate to white-collar chaos. Conflict takes the time and energy of those involved and distracts them from their priorities. In times of chaos, we cannot be effective. Our propensity to engage in controversy and to win contaminates our decisions. We are drawn to the tension of conflict and have trained ourselves to survive in the midst of turmoil.

Chaos in the boardroom exists in many forms. On the surface it may not be apparent. A company may appear to be operating in a controlled and sensible, business-as-usual existence. Yet, underneath the daily operation, an undertow of sabotage and confusion by the company's leadership may exist. This type of chaos can ultimately permeate an entire organization. The result is the inappropriate priority of independent agendas and a lack of harmony within the company.

Glaring examples of corporate chaos include the demise of *Fortune* 500 companies due to the hidden agendas of their CEOs and senior executives. Decisions to inflate revenues, hide debt, and distort bottom lines have placed many global business leaders in prison or at the very least cost them their livelihood. And subtler signs of chaos in the boardroom happen daily.

Perhaps your company faces the task of cost cutting. While each member of the executive committee is in agreement that the bottom line can be improved simply by eliminating luxury expenses, like flying private, first-class travel and country club memberships, no one wants to implement these cuts in their own department's budget. Ultimately, every manager operates from an autonomous view, each with his or her own independent agenda. The result is lack of teamwork, disharmony, and eventual chaos.

One way to eliminate chaos in the workplace is to notice the signs of mayhem as they evolve and react differently to the situation. By not engaging in the turmoil, you can promote clear thinking in your workplace. You may be aware of the chaos around you, but your mind, led by your kindness and values, rests in your acknowledgment of the circumstance without judgment.

Rather than reacting to the agenda of others, use the same amount of time and energy to access a place of non-duality where your heart and mind connect without an agenda. In this regard, you cannot be provoked by the chaos, but simply observe it as an expression of things as they are. In this quiet observation, the chaos is no longer stimulated or fed. Consequently, it is diluted to an anemic state and rendered ineffective. This process opens the gateway to creativity and productive events that maximize the real potential of your organization and its leadership.

In the example of cost cutting then, each manager would detach from the personal sacrifice that may arise from the task and simply appreciate the hardship that those involved will temporarily experience. By operating from a spirit of teamwork and compassion, the reward comes in the ultimate end result of improving the bottom line: saving jobs and strengthening the teamwork within the organization. This fearless act of doing what is right demonstrates true value-based leadership.

In chaos we do not settle our mind. Therefore, there is no rest, renewal, or replenishment. With inexhaustible tenacity, we stay fixed on a desired outcome, often numb to the damage we may be inflicting on the soul of the organization and on ourselves. Because we are passionate about the result, we think we are making progress. However, we may actually be creating an outcome that is quite the opposite of what we intended or desired.

The Buddha called this fixation on result "wanting mind." The wanting mind torments us primarily because there is never an end to the desire. Our wanting mind leaves us dissatisfied because it defines the existence of our company by what it does not have. We are stuck in mindset of *less than*, with an inability to access clarity. Craving to reach the end goal clogs our decisions.

Unfortunately, the goal has no end and therefore can never be obtained. Takuan Soho, a master of the Rinzai School of Zen in the early 1600s, once said, "The mind that does not stop at all is called immovable wisdom." We dilute our ability to access wisdom when we stir up the mind with unproductive chaos.

NO THOUGHT—HOW DOES THAT WORK?!

"Enlightenment is a state of wholeness . . . the end of the dreadful enslavement of incessant thinking."
—Eckhart Tolle

The undertow of anxiety that seems to coexist with the pressures of our careers is reliant on our view. Therefore, we have a choice. We can stay attached to our limited ideas, tightening around them, or we can give in to the possibility of new thoughts, or even more radical, *no thought*. Where does "no thought" fit into the speedy intelligence of corporate America? Actually, creating moments of no thought in the boardroom is essential to accessing the brilliant wisdom that innately resides there. Like the silence between the notes that create the music, moments of silence in boardroom communication provide the gap needed to access our primordial intelligence and achieve our goals.

By stepping away from a situation for a few minutes, we create a silence that is long enough to affect the challenge at hand. This process of creating "no thought" provides us with the ultimate space we need to find relief from the undertow of intensity and to rise to the surface without panic. Once on top and having relaxed in the moment, we are inspired to initiate the change needed for positive results.

FLUID THOUGHT

"Thoughts are as inherent to mind as waves are to water."
—The Buddha

When we surf, we cannot ride the same wave forever, just as we cannot cling to one thought. If our ideas are so prolific and ever changing, then why do we insist on holding on to those thoughts that keep us stuck? As leaders, we become more effective when we maintain a fluid mental state. This pliable mind keeps us creative and in the moment. We are more responsive to the needs of our organizations and can view circumstances with dexterity and fresh eyes. The fluidity evolves when we remove ourselves from our "me"-based bubble and begin to challenge our own thoughts. We no longer force one rigid solution, but rather, remain open to the possibility of a better idea.

CASE STUDY: RIGHT MINDFULNESS
SALESFORCE.COM

When Marc Benioff founded Salesforce.com in 1999, he may have been subliminally inspired by his own inherent ability to access Right Mindfulness.

Salesforce.com started from the position that the customers know what they want and need and that they should be able to manage and access the information in their business without spending millions of dollars for a complicated installed software system.

Benioff calls his strategy "the end of software," and this is where the connection with Right Mindfulness really begins. Since it is the luminous qualities of the mind that expand our creativity and enable us to tap into our highest potential, then who better to understand their real needs than the customers themselves? Benioff is providing a way to engage the minds of the customers in a fundamental and profitable way.

"Customers can build and customize the whole platform. That's something no one else is even trying. We're seeing customers build all kinds of new applications we couldn't have come up with. Customers are driving us in this direction," commented Benioff about his company's unique approach to Internet-driven technology.

This top-of-mind approach to customer resource management is paying off. The thriving business is averaging 7,500 new subscribers a month and annual revenues are exceeding $175 million.

Benioff is a complex individual, and his experience in mindfulness runs deeper than the vision of his business. A seasoned meditator, Benioff cultivated his vision of positively impacting society on a three-year journey traveling India. Highly invested in mental and sweat equity at his high-pressure sales and marketing job at Oracle, Benioff set out to explore the notion of enlightenment and learn about Eastern spirituality.

He returned with a solid meditation practice and the seed planted to create a way to pursue your dreams and give back to society—the basis for Right Mindfulness.

In July 2000, Benioff again tapped into his gift of Right Mindfulness and launched the Salesforce.com Foundation. Remembering the advice of a guru during his travels, Benioff realized his vision to give back to society. The Salesforce.com nonprofit arm provides technology and software to young people in disadvantaged communities around the world.

Benioff calls the foundation his "secret weapon. It's a great program, it does amazing work, but it also builds confidence in our employees," he says. "It makes people feel that this company is grounded. People learn that there's more out there than just themselves. When you talk to our employees, they say that they aren't here for the IPO. They're here because they want to be part of something big." Precisely the ground of the path of Right Mindfulness.

When we cultivate the ability to allow our thoughts to come and go by recognizing them simply as concepts, we actually widen our view. The tempo of our brain waves actually accelerates, and we increase our ability to lead with creativity. In essence, we expand our mind with multiple ideas rather than narrow it with an attachment to one thought. By letting go and allowing the fluidity of our thoughts to support us rather than own us, we can eventually ride the waves that will carry us to shore.

POWER IN THE PRESENT

Residing in the state of Right Mindfulness is only possible in the present. When we absorb the moment and are completely in the now, we become aware of our thoughts and feelings about everything that surrounds us and we experience. We are conscious. In this state of consciousness, we have the clarity to make choices. By disengaging from the conditioned chatter in our mind and staying in the present, we are able to make choices that come from our good intentions.

But how do we quiet this chatter, calm the mind, and soothe the soul in order to access the core of the moment? Are our minds actually in the way of ourselves and our own path to bottom-line enlightenment at work?

As discussed previously, our executive thoughts bind us to our egos and block us from what could be an effortless ability to communicate from the heart. When we learn to let go of the chatter of what, if, when, and how, we jump-start our mind to penetrate a spot of clarity. The most skillful way to stop the noise and detach from our thoughts is to be mindfully aware of them. We look at our thoughts as simply thoughts, acknowledge them as no more than that, and then disconnect their power from our own existence. Just like taking a break in a meeting, we are hitting the pause button within to find relief from the chatter in order to free the mind.

The process sounds simple, and yet it can be incredibly difficult and frustrating. We know that our thoughts at times can be our greatest tormentor. And yet, like an addictive relationship, we find it hard to disconnect and leave it. We get so caught up in our own thoughts that we virtually disengage ourselves from clarity. Yet, by committing to exploring the path of enlightenment, to being Buddha in the workplace, we gently begin to free ourselves by acknowledging our mental chatter. We catch our mind in its state of obsession over an issue, craving, or situation; say to ourselves, "just thinking, thinking"; let go of the thought; and move on. We do not criticize ourselves for the worry, as that in turn just gives more power to negativity. Instead, we gently accept our own humanness, knowing that the mind is only part of our whole being.

Staff Path Practice
Try this exercise during
your next executive
meeting.

Notice a moment when a discussion is heated and your colleagues are attached to their views. The conflict escalates and you sense the potential for an intellectual scuffle prompted by ego. In the peak of the moment, have the courage to suggest or request a silent break. Stop all conversations for 3 to 5 minutes. The participants can stay seated and remain silent.

If the situation is too intense, you can suggest a five-minute break from the room, but discourage use of the phone or e-mail that will only distract the mind. When you return to the conversation, notice the shift in the tension. Is it easier to make eye contact and breathe in the room? Can you offer levity and humor? You can further mitigate the stress in the room by verbally honoring the intention of the participants as they work toward solutions. Then provide new ground rules for continuing the discussion, such as:

1. Remind the participants that they are all included in the discussion because of the value that they bring to the group.

2. Ask that they only offer action-oriented ideas that are productive or provide a solution.

3. Decide that proposed solutions and ideas will be recorded and then reevaluated by the group in order of priority.

4. Ask the group to drop their pride of ownership of ideas and leave their egos at the door!

This process of observing and then letting go of our own thoughts disables the obsession to control things and run the show. It's as if the mind is nothing more than a character in a movie, a movie that we can pause, fast forward, rewind or eject all together. It does not manage our every existence or possess us, but it is simply a tool for us to help with the evolvement of our own inner path.

Developing the ability to connect mindfully with our awareness is very liberating. We are released from the prison of our fear-based thoughts and become free to go beyond our own intelligence. We let go of the controlling means of the mind and access our own inner wisdom, love, and creativity. In essence, we wake up! This release of the mind takes us to a space of higher awareness and a new state of alert clarity. We open to the possibilities of what the universe wants to offer us when we stop exclusively running the show.

RIGHT CONCENTRATION

> Mind moves, you return to stillness, but thus stilled, it moves all the more,
> while you persist in two extremes, how can you understand unity?
> —Seng-ts'an *Inscription on Trust in the Mind* (c. 600)

RIGHT CONCENTRATION

Buddhism is an experience rather than a belief. It is an expression of our authenticity and basic goodness as human beings. As the final aspect of the Eightfold Path, Right Concentration collects and unifies our focus and energy to enable us to relate directly to our experiences and the situation.

In business, it is this concentration that gives us the creative edge to access our wisdom in order to make the best decisions, on the spot. We are completely involved, absorbed in our company and the phenomenal world. This concentration is not forced but rather creative and natural.

Right Concentration is our intention to stay in the moment. At work, we merge Right View and Right Mindfulness to implement strategies and exceed our goals. Right Concentration is our training ground to perfect this merger and refine our ability to make good decisions with clarity and an awareness of their long-term implications. With conscious insight of what is really happening in the moment, we are inspired to communicate honestly and compassionately. We become present and aware, not just intellectually, but with a clear nonconceptual intelligence of what is really occurring in our companies.

As leaders, the more we train the mind to concentrate without condition, the more prolific we will be at accessing our wisdom. This is where pure, effective communication occurs. By engaging in Right Concentration, we set the pace for the lasting transformation of our organizations, not a quick, short-term fix.

RIGHT CONCENTRATION DIFFUSES OUR THOUGHTS

Like the waves of the ocean, there is no beginning or end to our thoughts. And just like the waves, all thoughts are different and occur at their exclusive and brief moment in time. As our thoughts come and go, some are so subtle that they may go unnoticed, while other thoughts can consume us.

Whether our thoughts are content or irritated, blissful or enraged, they still originate in our mind and remain there until we choose to act upon them. Understanding that our thoughts are without form, we can make a choice whether to act upon them or not. Our challenge then, is to accept each thought as a brief product of our intelligence and then to either take action or let it go.

Most of us place too much emphasis on our thoughts as they occur. Our propensity to hold on to them as if they are solid and real hampers our ability to make consistently good long-term decisions. For example, although your company is doing well, you fear may that it cannot last. Rather than concentrating on your excellent perfor-

Mindful Awareness
EXERCISE 21

These exercises will help you to train your mind to stay present.

- Place your mind in the boardroom or executive office and notice your first thought.
- Stay with the thought for as long as you can, noticing the pattern and subject of the thought. Is it subtle and indifferent? Is it intense, provoking an emotional connection?
- Now, try to let the thought go. Intentionally change the subject of the thoughts. Is this difficult to do? Does your mind want to wander back to the first subject of thought? Can you imagine the freedom of really being able to let go of that thought?

mance and thinking of ways to continue the upswing and generate even more revenue, you begin to pull back. Your mind has crept to a place of fear, and you begin to plan for tough days ahead. In your mind, you begin to conjure up a strategy to cut back or even lay off employees. These thoughts may be prudent, but more than likely they are self-defeating and unnecessary. The leader who is trained with Right Concentration may acknowledge the thoughts of fear, but will choose not to react to them. Rather, he will look at the thoughts and determine which are real and which are not. Then, through concentration, he will analyze his options of pulling back or pressing for greater performance and make a solid decision based upon all of the information that is available. By noticing the quality of our thoughts as they occur, we can—in a sharp and discerning way—choose whether to act upon them or ignore them. This discrimination frees us of the compulsive tendency to react to every thought through emotion. We can finally step off of our mental treadmill and explore the freshness of a new, uncluttered way of thinking.

MEDITATION FOR RIGHT CONCENTRATION

The path of Right Concentration leads to the highest form of wakefulness by cultivating an awareness of every thought, every emotion, every action, and every word that stems from that thought. How can we develop our mind to create this razor sharp quality? Single-pointed concentration, a form of secular meditation, offers us a healthy and effective tool to train in strengthening our awareness.

The skillful art of meditation provides you with the spaciousness needed to make the right choices and exercise your complete intellectual capacity. The practice of daily meditation releases our need to control a situation and enables us to look at it with fresh eyes. When you sit quietly in meditation for a few minutes daily, you move toward clarity and simplicity of thought. You are able to access your intuitive, compassionate side, looking at decisions with patience and wisdom.

Cutting-edge CEOs across America such as William Clay Ford, Jr., of Ford Motor Company; Pierre Omidyar, founder of eBay; and Marc Benioff of Salesforce.com have all discovered the immense benefits of a regular meditation practice. Meditation provides vitality and clarity to leaders in all industries, each of which has its own unique pressures. Whether it is Eileen Fisher, Founder and CEO of Eileen Fisher, designing functional and flattering apparel for women; David Orlinsky, Vice Chairman of NetJets, Inc., shuttling heavy hitters to meetings around the nation or Peter D. Mandelstam, president and founder of Arcadia Windpower Ltd., developing wind electricity for global construction projects, each understands the benefits of a regular meditation practice.

By starting your day with a simple meditation practice, you are setting the intention for what the day will bring. Just like a regular exercise program, the healthy benefits of your practice can extend throughout your day and week. Unlike exercise, you can do this practice anywhere, on the edge of your bed, on the train during your commute, or in a chair at your desk.

Launching Your Meditation Practice

By now you may have decided to introduce meditation into your daily routine or to determine if it is for you. Begin with a basic form of meditation that uses the simple breath as the object of your meditation. The simple and most direct form of meditation is to focus on the breath. By directing your attention to your breath, you have a place to put your thoughts. This focus on the breath slows down your mind and takes your attention inward.

The following is a basic meditation instruction that can enhance a daily well-being routine for busy executives:

1. Sit with feet hip-distance apart and flat on the floor.

(continued on following page)

2. Check for an erect alignment of your body from the head to the shoulders and down to your hips. Rest your arms at your sides or fold your hands effortlessly in your lap.
3. Gaze four to five feet in front of you. Hold the position of your mouth relaxed and slightly open, with your tongue resting softly on the roof of your mouth.
4. Breathe in and breathe out, noticing only the breath and allowing the nourishment of the breath itself to cleanse your spirit.
5. As thoughts come up (which they will), acknowledge their presence as just thoughts and then let them go, returning to the breath.
6. As you breathe, with a natural breathing pace, you will begin to release all anxiety, judgment, and worry.

In the beginning, you may find that you are able to engage in this exercise only for a minute or two. You sit, you begin to stir, your mind gets speedy, and you think that you are failing at the simple exercise of focusing on the breath. This discovery can be quite humbling for CEOs and executives who consider themselves adept at mental challenge.

Some of the obstacles that you may encounter with the practice of meditation involve the sheer physical challenges of just sitting and placing your body in a disciplined posture. Also, in the early stages of meditation, many people experience physical discomfort as their bodies learn to adapt to holding the posture without movement. You may become restless, and if you choose to sit on a meditation cushion, you may feel discomfort in your hips, or perhaps your feet might fall asleep. These sensations are quite normal and eventually diminish as your body settles down and adapts to sitting.

By doing this exercise for a few minutes each day, you are harnessing your stressed-out mind and replenishing your body with health and vitality. Ultimately, your communication with others is more effective, as you see the world from a wider point of view. Free of clutter and grasping on to a particular outcome, you articulate your thoughts with clarity. Your mind focuses on what is important as you peel away the distractions. Less obsessed with taking shortcuts to obtain an outcome, you begin to appreciate the process. You also appreciate time itself.

With continued practice, you are able to surrender to the breath with greater ease. Each session may be extended by a minute or so. Your mind takes hold of itself. Your priority in the moment is no more than to enjoy the breath itself. You are cleansed and freed of worry. You are revitalized with appreciation of just your breath. You can call upon this practice anytime that you feel anxiety or confusion or feel the need to sharpen your concentration.

RIGHT CONCENTRATION OF TIME

Just as we would like to have the ability to forecast the weather, so would we like to control time, yet neither is possible. As His Holiness The Dalai Lama reminds us, "Time never waits." That is our only certainty about time.

Time as a tangible form is simply a tool to organize each moment, week, and year. Yet, time itself is not solid and is really nothing more than thought. How then does it maintain such tight control over our lives? Is time the barometer of our existence, or is it simply an instrument to help keep us focused and organized?

Chogyam Trungpa Rinpoche, a meditation master and teacher well known for bringing Buddhist philosophies to our Western society, used to say that he always showed up at the perfect time, regardless of what time it was! Trungpa Rinpoche was awake, in the present, and enlightened. He was said to have mastered the art of timing his presence and his teachings to make the most impact. What an amazing sales tool that would be in today's modern business world!

On one level we resist time and the process of aging, and yet simultaneously, we seem to be rushing it, keenly aware that it never waits. We compete with time to develop new products, to be the first to market or leverage the stock market for the greatest return. This conflict of time is one of our greatest koans—something that we can contemplate that will lead us to reflect on the deeper truths of life.

Time gives us the security of change and, likewise, the insecurity of change. We have peace of mind in knowing that everything changes, an inner awareness that acknowledges that there is nothing to grasp on to. And yet, even with this knowledge we still grasp on to time itself.

The path of Right Concentration helps to tether your appreciation and fear of time. A great deal of spiritual material in recent years focuses on the concept of staying in the moment. Staying in the moment can provide a luminous quality that delivers clarity and glimmers of enlightenment. However, if the concept of being in the now does not include a respect for time itself, you run the risk of floating in a lofty space of existence void of any sense of urgency, which is not realistic for today's deadline-driven global marketplace.

The concept of time plays such a large role in our day-to-day existence at work. Our computers, watches, e-mail, and electronic organizers navigate our meetings and activities moment by moment. And yet, the mind continues to wander. That is because the mind is not controlled by time. Our thoughts, feelings, and perceptions are time-bound, but the mind remains free to wander, digress, project, and deny.

Herein lays the dilemma of time itself. By developing Right Concentration, we are able to rest in the present and sharpen our own inner clarity. Since time never waits, we must cultivate awareness for both the use of time and the preciousness of the present moment. We are keenly aware of both the power and fragility of the now.

This awareness of time ultimately improves the quality of each moment as we practice our daily lives with an ardent desire to heighten our experience of the present moment.

FREE-FALLING IN THE MOMENT

When we are present, in the now, we experience an unencumbered freedom to be ourselves. We know who we are and can fearlessly express our beliefs and ambitions. This confidence ultimately goes beyond the realm of ourselves and touches the lives of those with whom we work in a like-minded contagious way.

Right Concentration provides the view to take risks essential to success. As leaders who are training in meditation and strengthening our ability to be present, we have confidence in the positive results of our efforts. Our decisions come from a secure place of strength as we trust our intuition, close our eyes, and jump—without looking back. We have developed the skill to stay present and focused on our vision as we free-fall in the moment. Whether we develop strategic business plans, upgrade product portfolios, or enter a new marketplace, our safety net against failure rests in our passion to for the process and our ability to stay present.

In competitive business climates, every minute counts. There is a sense of urgency to build a brand or business that ignites internal enthusiasm and relentless team effort.

Whether you start up a business, compete in a marathon, or bring a product to market, the race against time is invigorating and intense. By employing Right Concentration, you create an immediacy of time to improve the quality of your work and to raise your bottom line.

The task of balancing your strength and ambition with gentle humility requires communicating from the heart. By staying soft and

Mindful Awareness
EXERCISE 22

Consider these questions to increase your focus of Right Concentration:

- What aspects of your job bring you up against time most frequently?
- What images can you rely on to bring you back to the present moment? Who or what in your life brings you immediately into the present?
- Recall the times when you were completely present in business. How were they different than settling for a quick fix? Did you find greater clarity to make decisions?

continuously checking in to make sure that your intention is genuine, you will do the right thing, make the right decisions, and ultimately succeed.

COMMITMENT TO CONSCIOUS AWARENESS

Commitment is more than being dedicated to your company, organization, or goal. In the mindset of the Buddha, commitment involves a realization of your true potential. By acknowledging your gifts of compassion and insight, you can rest in a space of inner stillness. Once in that state, freed of your external desires for more power, money, or control, you find comfort in the commitment to being the best you can be. This awakened freedom provides a new meaning to the concept of achievement.

Our success now lies in our ability to access our unfulfilled potential. Before we can access this potential, we must have the courage to look within and challenge our own motivations, values and business practices. We must lean into the edge of the sword.

STAYING FLUID AND RESOLVING CONFLICT

Entranced in contemplation,
Provoked by the ebb and flow of the changing tide
I inhale a flicker of now
And exhale a reflective goodbye to the same moment . . .
One breath . . . one wave
Awake to the perpetual impermanence of each
—Peaking before groundlessness
A call to let go . . .

As you engage in the process of letting go, your logic tells you to avoid or ignore thoughts that create angst. Yet, the more you try to avoid them, the more solid they become. The only solution for removing the anxiety is to confront it head-on and sit with it.

Yet, when we are in crisis, challenged by competitive earnings, internal conflicts, or stockholder concerns, we seldom have the time to delay a decision long enough to explore every dimension of the situation. With a strong sense of urgency, we address the issue too quickly and seek solutions. Frequently, the solutions that we implement only provide Band-Aids for the symptoms at hand rather than a final resolution of the issue.

If, on the other hand, we can strategically examine the actual source of the conflict, we position our organizations and ourselves for greater long-term, bottom-line results.

Most conflict, whether business or personal, usually stems from desire and emotion. We have the desire to improve profitability, to increase productivity, to be first to market. All of these seemingly tactical goals are fueled by our own internal human emotion—perhaps fear of losing our jobs, a sense of competitiveness, or insecurity about our intelligence and our skills. And with that emotion comes pressure, angst, and attachment.

By getting in touch with the source of your anxiety and transferring that tension to productive, positive efforts, you begin to operate from a position of personal power. You shift the very core of your attention to a new, pithier style of leadership. You will find relief in your ability to acknowledge the source of the conflict, while not buying into the emotional burden that typically comes with conflict. Rather, you acknowledge the conflict as thought and use your feelings associated with the discomfort to stay flexible.

By not giving into fear, ego, anger, or other typical defense patterns, we allow ourselves to stay open and receptive to new growth possibilities. With Right Concentration, we can capture the fundamental Buddha nature of our organization and ultimately create a healthy, fluid, resilient company with long-term sustainability.

THERE IS NO WALL!

Kelly, a senior executive and twenty-five-year veteran with a major television network, decided to run the Big Sur marathon. Prior to this decision, the longest distance that he had ever run was ten miles. But

Staff Path Practice

This practice integrates many of the lessons that have been worked with throughout the paths of this book.

Strategic: Ask your staff if they could fast forward the company by three years, in what state would they like for it to be? What products have been launched? What is the size of the workforce? What would the press write about their contributions to the community?

Tactical: Now, ask the staff to mentally return to the immediate moment and ask the same questions in the present sense. Are their products that you need in order to compete? Is your workforce productive? What would the press say about your company's community contributions today?

Operational: Compare the wish list for the company of the future to the company as it is today. Identify where it is realistic to make the changes. Then, as a group, agree on the top three changes that they can help to implement over the next three, six, and twelve months. Assign timelines to these goals and employees to manage the efforts.

Kelly needed a good challenge—one that would take his mind off his intense job and the cutthroat politics of the broadcast business.

The marathon runner's favorite mantra is "there is no wall." Even at the peak of their training and fitness levels, many marathon runners have experienced the knotty phenomenon of hitting the wall. Whether this mental trap lasts for a few steps or several miles, the excruciating test of endurance brings up a struggle between body and mind that can go either way. They can finish the race or cave into their tired bodies and minds and quit.

In the Buddhist tradition, there is a similar test of endurance called the "dathun." Essentially, this intensive practice involves "sitting," or meditating, for thirty days. Day after day, week after week, the participant sits on the meditation cushion from about 7 A.M. until 9 P.M. Moment by moment, the practitioner strives to become one with his or her breath, as the physical, and often mental, pain escalates. The mantra? "Be the breath." Sounds simple enough, but given the choice, many would choose to run a marathon before engaging in this excruciating test of endurance between body and mind.

Just like the marathon runner, there is nothing but the mind to stand in the way of meditating for thirty straight days. Each and every thought that arbitrarily pops into the meditator's mind can make or break the completion of the thirty-day mind training session. Just like the runner, the meditator does his best not to go there—not to succumb to the temptation to quit. What is the key to success in both situations? *Nothing. No thought.* Keep your mind focused on one thing: the breath. Sound simple? Try it if you haven't already. Focus only on your breath and attempt to count to ten without thought. Each time a thought of any flavor enters your mind, begin your count again. Engaging in this simple exercise could drive you to begin training for a runner's marathon.

Once you are over the hump and have broken through the imaginary wall, whether it is mile marker twenty or day twenty into your sit, you are rewarded with tidbits of tools that seem like oceans of pleasure. In the run, you may be handed a glass of water, tossed a health bar, or applauded by the crowds on the sidelines, who know that you are close to the finish line. In meditation, you are given permission to actually look at your thoughts, but with limited regularity. You are handed the gift of contemplative meditation, giving you the long-awaited permission to place your mind on a specific image or concept to yield fruitful thoughts that will hopefully take you one step closer to enlightenment.

As both the meditator and the marathon runner cross their finish lines, they both know that the end is just the beginning. After all, each goal, each challenge is simply a product of thought. In Kelly's case, he placed his mind in a moving meditation to finish the race. And for the meditator, the challenge of sitting shifts to a deeper connection to the present with each day of practice. Magically, once finished with their respective challenges, feeling weary, yet exuding greater strength and confidence, both the runner and the meditator usually begin searching for their next race, their next program, whether on the trail or on the cushion. In Kelly's case, through his discipline and trained mind, I predict that he can set a personal record pace for either.

CULTIVATING EQUANIMITY

We are all in training, regardless of our level of accomplishment, financial success, or achievement. Whether we occupy a seat on the U.S. Senate, sit on the board of directors of a major corporation, work in Wal-Mart as a checkout clerk, or pick up trash for Waste Management, we all still feel, dream, and love. We also all seek avenues of relief from sorrow and pain.

Recognizing that we are all on the same playing field of humanity is the first step in thinking larger than ourselves. When we look at the world in this capacity of oneness, we see that there is no real separation. All humans are interconnected, all on an equal level when it comes to the heart, regardless of our level of evolvement.

This is a difficult concept to grasp when we consider the harsh extremes of mankind and motivation that exist on the planet. How can there be such corruption, hate, and disparity in a world that also delivers the exquisite surround of an ocean-front sunset and the love of parents for a newborn child. Examples are endless, yet each provides us with the raw fuel to step away from the immediate desire to live in our habitual patterns and obtain one immediate goal after another.

By being aware of the extremes in an experience or emotion, you can use the juxtaposition to measure your attachments and learn to let go. Buddhist principles consider the obsession for these opposite extremes as obstacles of our growth toward enlightenment. When you exist in an extreme space of pleasure or pain, gain or loss, hope or fear, you in effect block your ability to experience the whole of life. How can you really know what sadness is or relate to it in others if you are perpetually happy? Though we often wish for happiness, experiencing it without suffering at all would cut us off from the rest of humanity, and we would never overcome dualistic thinking. Suffering is in fact a blessing!

Your job then is to go a level deeper, identify with the emotion itself and recognize that the same feelings of fear, sadness, and loss exist in others. It is only with this recognition that you experience true compassion and true loving kindness and taste the relief of equanimity. With Right Concentration, you have the confidence to function from an unlimited position of loving kindness.

When you access this sacred spot of your intelligence, you are unencumbered and connected to your core values. You are vividly present and positioned to lead your organization with a sharp mind. Right Concentration keeps us focused on the view and strengthens our abilities to communicate from the heart.

When we begin to cultivate equanimity, we depersonalize the process and the result. From a compassionate point of view, we begin to appreciate the accomplishments and efforts of others, including our competitors.

CONCLUSION
THE RIGHT CORPORATION

> "We begin to find that we are searching too much . . .
> In the end we never find a mate . . . ."
> —Chogam Trungpa Rinpoche, *Cutting Through Spiritual Materialism*

BOTTOM LINE: WHAT DO YOU REALLY NEED?

How many times in the course of a week do you find yourself thinking, "When I (blank), I'll be happy." When I launch this product, I'll take my vacation. When we make our plan, I can relax. When we grow the business to X, I will slow down. When I am promoted to X, I will have arrived. When our stock hits $$$, we will acquire XYZ . . . "

For most of us, the "whens" never really end. They roll over in our minds like investments of consciousness to benchmark our progress and validate our self-worth. We incessantly search for the next opportunity for accomplishment. This search keeps us hooked into our story line.

October and November are always bittersweet months in the marketing business. Entering the last quarter of the fiscal year provides agencies the home stretch opportunity to exceed planning and realize the remaining sales possibilities of the year. With one eye on the budget and another on the eventual bonuses that I would have the pleasure of giving to many well-deserving employees, every October I would begin to apply year-end pressure to maximize revenues and control year-end costs.

Simultaneously with the sales push, we were developing the budget and plan for the following fiscal year. As the weeks clicked away and we drew close to the year end, knowing that we were certain to make or exceed our annual plan, the feelings of success and accomplishment were diluted. Our attention had already turned to the next year and upcoming tasks at hand. We left little, if any, space or time for celebration.

Invariably, the next year's plan was more aggressive than we would have liked and usually felt a bit out of our comfort zone. The glass ceiling of success continued to rise higher, year after year, with no end in sight.

This scenario is common to many businesses, whether small or global in size. When goals are based solely upon the shareholders' return or increased net profits, something is missing. The company is left with a hole in its soul. Like a dancer staring over the shoulder of her partner in hopes of spotting a more attractive mate, the relentless CEO always searches for the next deal. Sadly in the end, she never finds her mate.

In this mindset of perennial fiscal growth, we can never have enough, which is the greatest irony of all. Once on top, we yearn to go back to simplicity and indulge in nothing more than the spaciousness found hidden quietly within. So we retreat for a week or two to a beach and a book in search of that lost simplicity. This Band-Aid provides only temporary relief.

Wouldn't it be satisfying to access that gentle simplicity at a moment's notice? As Buddha in the workplace or the boardroom, you can ease off of the climb long enough to reacquaint yourself with your tender heart. How?

Begin by establishing a meditation practice. Next, set aside a time to get off of the treadmill long enough to reevaluate your vision, integrity, and values. Introspectively check in with this exercise on a quarterly and annual basis, and see how well you are holding to your mission.

Finally, explore new ways to reward and give back. What are your passions and those of your organization? Is it the environment, children's issues, or a health-related cause? The number of causes to support are endless. Yet, you will find a greater reward from your support and giving than perhaps from your own increased prosperity.

Seasoned givers such as Jeff Swartz, Marc Benioff, and Oprah Winfrey are just a few examples of corporate philanthropy that has come full circle.

Right Concentration that is enhanced by generosity can actually stimulate your leadership drive and motivate your employees. Shifting the focus from "me" to "them" in an any organization will also help to minimize turnover, increase productivity, and drive up profitability.

THE ACQUISITIONIST CLIMB

We spend years in undergraduate and graduate schools to earn the coveted degree, MBA, or title that will prepare us to climb the ladder to success. Step by step, we conform to an old model of business, a traditional one that is based solely upon profitability. Before the breakout of the corporate accounting scandals and recession that followed, few questioned the validity or sustainability of these business doctrines. Now leaders and consumers realize that successful career lives are not based solely upon increasing the shareholders' profit. However, the paradigm shift toward ethics and values has been in a slow transition.

Managers throughout America are still being groomed for success in a traditional sense as they climb the ladder with credentials in hand, keeping a keen eye focused on the pot of profitably at the top. Preoccupation with "making it" hazes over our access to clarity as we create a cloud of confusion based upon our obsession with obtaining the next title and increasing profit margins. We are not content or settled within, but we keep on climbing as if increasing our credentials and acquisitions will numb the angst of the incomprehensible thought of not making it.

The irony is that as we strategically build barriers to protect ourselves and climb to reach our goals, we are also building barricades

Mindful Awareness
EXERCISE 23

For a moment, consider your life to be an actual corporation. In your imagination, place your entire being into a boardroom setting.

- What lessons and milestones have shaped your company's identity and success?
- Recall the major events that propelled your company to new heights. What vision and goals prompted that growth?
- Now take this practice to your staff. Ask them the same questions.

between our accomplishments and our authentic self. We have won the race to "success" and lost ourselves in the process.

By treating your life as a living, breathing corporation, you can position yourself to operate with a higher quality of wakefulness. With dignity and integrity, you can transform how you work, live, and invest your energy.

As you evaluate your life's direction and strategies for the next decade and beyond, what will motivate you to continue to sharpen your personal operating system and moral standards?

CEOs throughout corporate America are discovering the integration of spirituality into the workplace. On the heels of the trillion-dollar information technology age and fueled by corporate scandals and mistrustful shareholders, we are experiencing a grassroots movement of CEOs, leaders, and managers who bring ethics and morality into business. Landmark books such as *Cultural Creatives*, *The Power of Now*, and *The Purpose-Driven Life* support this spiritual epidemic to turn inward in order to outwardly transform how we do business and conduct our lives.

The mindful implementation of the Eightfold Path for business delivered in *Buddha: 9 to 5* provides the core practice to help you consciously wake up your organization. The approach is inward as you introspectively analyze current motives and values. It then becomes outward as you experience the inspiration and application of emerging wakefulness.

As you engage in the process, you will discover that you are in good company as the spiritual core of corporate America continues to mushroom. This trend is coming full circle as millions of managers, investors, business leaders, and consumers choose the high road.

As the practice shifts from personal and inward to external and into the institution, you may find yourself in new business circles of like-minded managers who choose to connect with those who also lead their organizations with a higher consciousness. These relationships offer the connections and mental equity to form your own personal board of directors who will support your socially responsible bottom line.

BUDDHA'S PERSONAL BOARD OF DIRECTORS

Who you associate with is fundamental to your continued growth and accomplishments. Surrounding yourself with like-minded leaders, family, and friends who genuinely care about your well-being and embrace your mission and values is essential to fulfilling your vision and nurturing your total well-being.

As the Buddha and chairman of your company, who do you want to invite onto your board of directors to help you fulfill a complete life experience that realizes your dreams? Consider the aspects of your personal organization that need to be polished or perhaps even reengineered. Is your personal asset portfolio as organized and strategic as the profit and loss statement for your business? Do you need to place more emphasis on your health, your recreation, and your family? What about your spiritual and community life? Are you engaged in your community and actively creating opportunities to give back?

By forming your own personal board, which is different from your company's existing board, you strategically acquire the support that you need to balance your life and position yourself to reap the rewards of your daily effort and action.

Use the mandala (found in the next section) to identify the primary principles of your life and insert the names of those friends or colleagues you would like to offer a board seat. What will you require of your board members? Primarily, you will want them to provide you with honest feedback and to support your mission of vision and service to the world. You may also require that your board members interdependently work building mutually beneficial support systems. In this regard, you collaborate and grow, building an organization that is focused on a bottom line that gives to each other and enhances the world.

THE AWAKE CEO

In the midst of an ineffective, conventional career model, there emerges a bold new crop of CEOs who stake new ground and take both profitability and social responsibility to heart. These CEOs of all ages are doing the inward work essential to create the kind of outward change that will awaken corporate America.

Bill George, the former chairman and CEO of Medtronic, mastered the art of being *Buddha: 9 to 5*. By integrating wisdom with compassion, he meditates and motivates himself and his employees to stay focused on their mission to be recognized as a company of dedication, honesty, integrity, and service. Their overarching goal, "To maintain good citizenship as a company," is exceeded year after year.

Socially responsible leaders know that wherever they go, they are the Buddha. Charged and inspired to be the "Right Person," they own the responsibility that comes with enlightened leadership. Starbucks blends its products with their desire to do good work, and the wisdom to impact positively the lives of its employees and customers. Daily decisions are made with an eye toward their mission: "to provide a great work environment and treat each other with respect and dignity."

These practices become the catalyst for an entirely new brand of management, one based upon integrity and values that will survive the eventual shakedown of capitalism as we once knew it, and insist that companies give back to their employees.

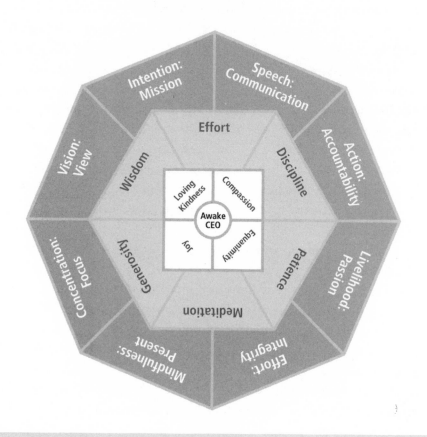

THE AWAKE EMPLOYEE

With the low rate of unemployment in the United States and the recent exposure of immoral leadership, today's employees are exercising discriminating vision about whom they wish to work for. The talented workforce in this country has a choice, and their employment decisions are demonstrating their preference to perform for people-based organizations. A year-long study conducted by McKinsey & Company reflects that employee talent will be the single most important corporate resource over the next twenty years. Their famous "War for Talent" study confirms that the scrimmage for the best and the brightest people has become the corporate war of today.

Prosperity and the bottom line are dependent upon employee performance, and today's workforce is selecting companies that offer a value-driven culture that is conscious and cares about more than just its growing profit margin. While profitability and growth are essential to the survival of business, the path of *Buddha: 9 to 5* shows us how spirit at work can increase productivity and profitability on many levels. Larry, the CEO of a major telecommunications company, stated, "At the end of the day, we bet on people, not strategies." This boardroom battlefield is vulnerable and tenacious. Retention of qualified employees who have been in their companies for three to ten years becomes slippery as they begin to feel unappreciated and explore other employment options. The battle for good talent has escalated the attrition rates as companies are raiding each other for top producers. Employees want to place their talents with great companies that make a difference in the world.

What keeps an employee loyal in these competitive times? According to the McKinsey report, great companies are "those that are well managed, that have terrific values, and a great culture." The principles of *Buddha: 9 to 5* fill these requirements by designing awake companies that deliver morality, room to grow, and appreciation for performance. This appreciation reveals itself from the top down as enlightened CEOs strive to connect with their workforce one on one, making them feel that they are contributors to the enterprise. That wisdom-based connection transfers from the employer to the employee and cements the loyalty that will preserve the primary commodity essential to the prosperity of an organization—its people. The phenomenon of cultivating multigenerational Buddha-minded employees creates the priceless and essential transformation of a long-term flourishing corporate culture.

SHARING THE REALITY OF CHANGE

Buddhist terms such as suffering, egolessness, impermanence, equanimity, and karma are expressions of one master truth in the grandest view—our reality. Whether you are a seasoned manager or new to your position, your reality will eventually cross the same path with the reality of everyone else in your life. You may be working with another manager to negotiate a huge product acquisition that will change your company's future or simply sharing the same shade under a cloud with a stranger. The situation is only the momentary container for the relationship that exists between you and another at a particular point in time. The reality of who we are and how we conduct ourselves leads to one core basic truth for each and every one of us: We are always in relationship. The acknowledgment of this coexistence can replace the burden of what once was known as top-down management and decisions based solely on profitability. Rather, we are in this world together, socially conscious and aware of our mutual responsibility to drive ethical change, and that knowledge provides comfort.

Knowing that we share a common ground with each and every person with whom we come in contact, even if that common ground is that we are both at the same place in the same time, helps to soften the edges of our intense lives.

When we move this truth to the workplace, we can muster up thoughts of acceptance for even the most irritating colleague or ruthless competitor. The reality of common ground takes the focus off of "me" long enough to exhibit concern for another, long enough to create space, a gap from our own hopes and fears. We detach, if only for a split second, from our own solid egos.

Because dharma is reality, it blankets all of life, including our jobs. This reality originates from mind itself and encompasses our total experience: our needs, desires, fears, aspirations, guilt, anger, and so on. As the Buddha at work or in the boardroom, you can understand this common ground and make decisions that touch the well-being and prosperity of your employees.

It is said that all dharmas agree on one point: "The concern for others." We can use this consensus in our work environment as a basis for our own interactions. By consciously relating to others, we apply practice in action. Each day when you arrive at work, take a few minutes to remind yourself to show genuine consideration for another. Ask others about their friends and relatives, their pets, or how their weekend went. Watch the change in how employees relate to you when the emphasis of the moment shifts from you to them.

Likewise, during your next conversation with a customer, ask her questions that are about her life, unrelated to business, and observe the difference in communication. You may receive a friendlier, less defensive response once your client senses your genuine interest.

These small gestures of kind-heartedness are the seeds of generosity that will grow your business to epic performance. Once the ground is planted with the Eightfold Path and the seeds of generosity germinate and bloom, they will spread throughout your organization like brilliant fireweed in a summer pasture.

GENEROSITY TO IMPROVE THE BOTTOM LINE

What is the real bottom line of all of this mind and heart training and bringing Buddha into the boardroom? Where does the compassion (the rubber) really meet society (the road)?

When we consider the biggest view—a healthy, peaceful planet—it is easy to think about being generous. We all acknowledge that we want to give back. It is our moral obligation. But when? When we make a certain amount of millions or retire at a specific age?

Generosity is a mindset that is accessible at any time. It's not contingent upon a benchmark or goal. It is there for us to tap into as simply as we inhale a sweet scent or feel the delight of a cool breeze. In the Buddha's world, generosity is a primary characteristic of being an "awake being," someone who is dedicated to helping and awakening others. The act of generosity keeps us connected to others and helps us to let go of our selfish preoccupation. When we give, we intuitively stop grasping to what is "ours," putting our self-indulgence on hold.

Sometimes this is not that easy. Even when we try to consider others first, we can get in our own way. We create a false or conditional sense of giving tied to what we ultimately will get out of our own act of generosity. Our preprogrammed survival tools to take care of number one block the access to our own hearts. We get stuck on what we don't have, what we need, and what will make us feel better.

When we catch ourselves in this limited, self-centered mindset, we are given an opportunity to shift a very small, closed view to a much larger view of generosity. Rather than thinking about what it is we don't have, we can visualize someone else being happy and in good health. This subtle shift in thought injects the moment with levity and allows us to move away from the pain or frustration of our own thoughts.

When I ran my company, I would frequently use the morning commute time to think about how and what I could give at work that day. Mentally, I would scan the faces of my employees and customers, focusing on the individuals who could use a good dose of kindness and joy. Admittedly, this was not an everyday occurrence because I would also engage in my own habitual thoughts of landing an account or expanding a sale. But when my attention centered on helping others, I would have the best time with it and arrive at work excited and inspired. I would then enter the company with my bag of mental goodies, using them to touch others and to ignite the day.

Sometimes the resulting acts would billow with large intent, like calling a meeting to announce a new incentive plan or company trip as a gesture of thanks for the hard work done. Other times the acts were much subtler, like thanking an assistant for doing an especially nice job on a project. Or I would drop a note to a loyal client and offer a personal thought of thanks and gratitude for their business.

This same spirit of generosity seemed to perpetuate throughout my organization. While many of our competitors charged for their time, we charged by the project, with the intent to always give our clients more than they expected.

While this style of doing business in the marketing industry can create an exhausting daily agenda, it also proved to be fulfilling. Often, we would work grueling hours to exceed our client's expectations. Once, I had an Olympic client, for whom we had completed a project in a very short amount of time, comment, "What, do you have a bunch of elves running around here at night?"

The staff felt so good about the job that they had done as a result of that comment that it made them want to do more work for the client. Their generosity of time and energy, in their minds, had been rewarded by her appreciation.

On a daily basis, our acts of generosity need not be monumental. Giving a coworker a bit more attention to really hear how his weekend went or closing down e-mail during a phone call to really hear what the other person is saying are subtle yet significant gestures of giving in the moment.

By placing our attention on the needs of others, we become free to think and feel clearly and unencumbered. It is this spaciousness that propels our creativity to a new level. We can now make decisions that offer greater reward for all concerned—not just ourselves. In this regard, the gift of generosity actually improves the bottom line!

SILENCE MEETS SERVICE

Once you reach a pinnacle of success and wealth, a sense of philanthropy and giving back to society begins to heighten. Our goals and ambitions shift. Our increased means enable us to give back on a level that will make a prosperous impact on the planet. We look within again and evaluate what is most important. But this time we are relating from a basis of values and less from one of abundance. We choose a cause that motivates us from the soul, and the work begins again.

The beauty of the process is that the giving often becomes just the catalyst for the next evolution of prosperity. By attaching to a cause and giving of our time, talents, and money, we find ourselves stimulated by a newfound creativity. We are back in the game, with new players and an open field freshly groomed for new phases of generosity.

When we ask ourselves, "What do I really need," we are met with a new and profound challenge. We look inside and initiate a new process—one of simplifying to strengthen. We return to the path of *Buddha: 9 to 5*, let go, and come back to the stillness that reflects who we really are.

Having initiated the path to waking up, we come back with fresh eyes and insights. It is those insights that improve our real bottom line. We redefine our purposes and realize that what we really need is simply time—time to enjoy the treasures of our own discovery and the peace that resides within.

INDEX